I0468116

Centered Coloring

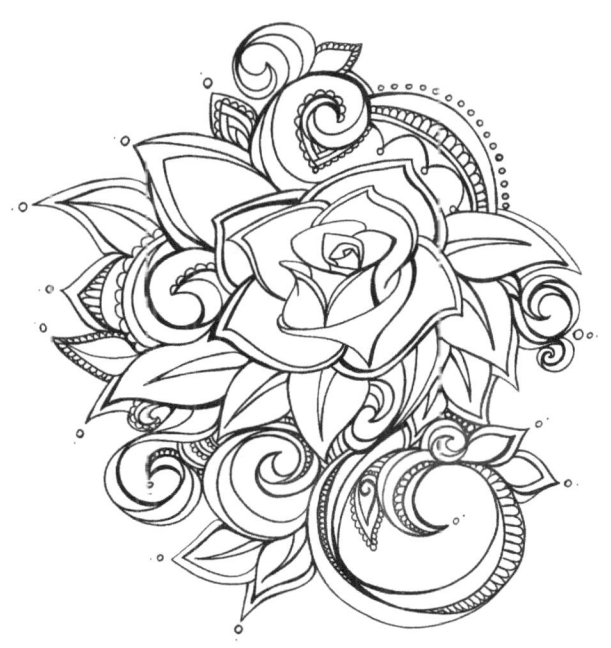

Heather Hausenfleck Middleton

http://centeredcoloring.com

Centered Coloring
Copyright 2016, Heather Hausenfleck Middleton

Arranged for print by No Cube Press
http://nocubepress.com

ISBN: 1530662141
ISBN-13: 978-1530662142

Download additional pages to print at home

http://centeredcoloring.com

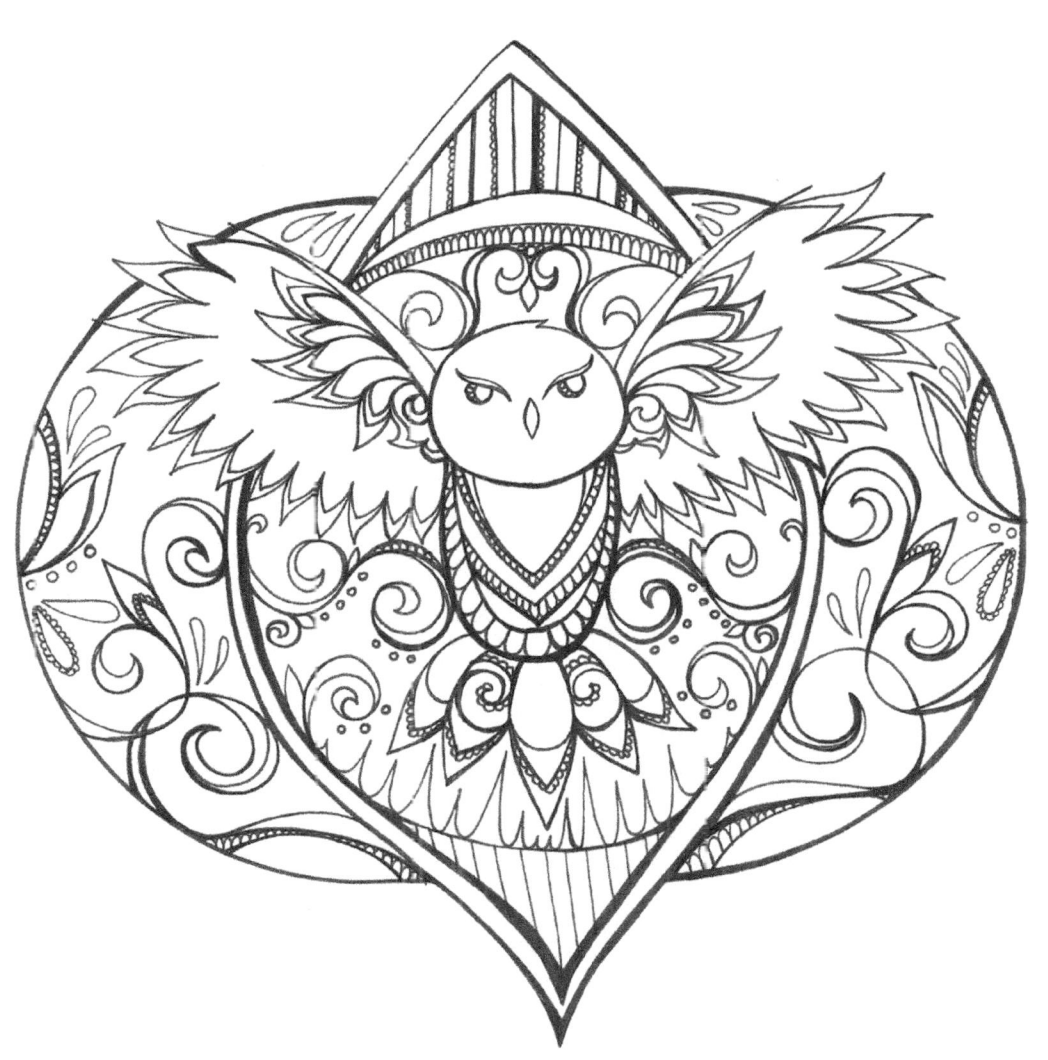

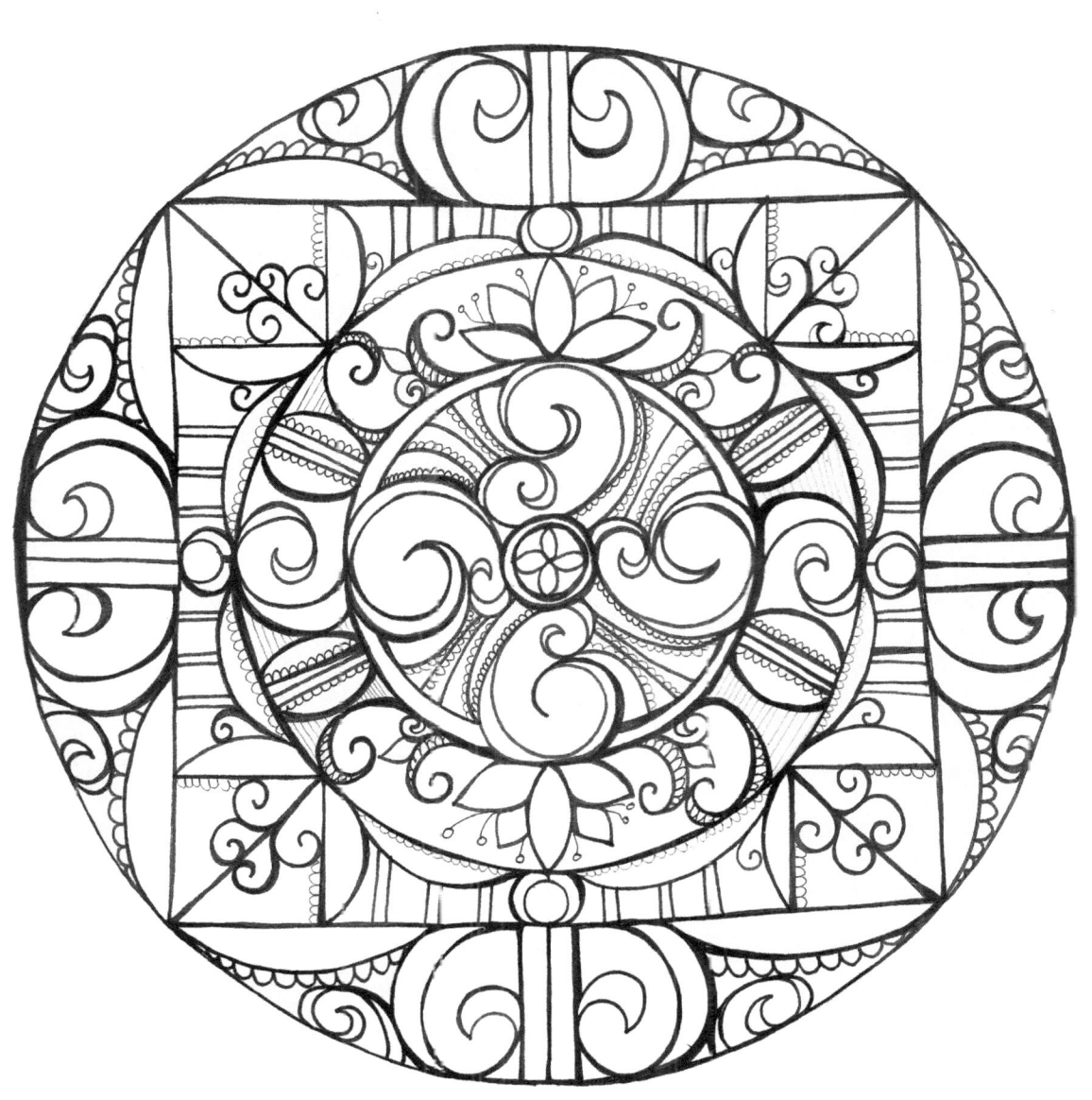

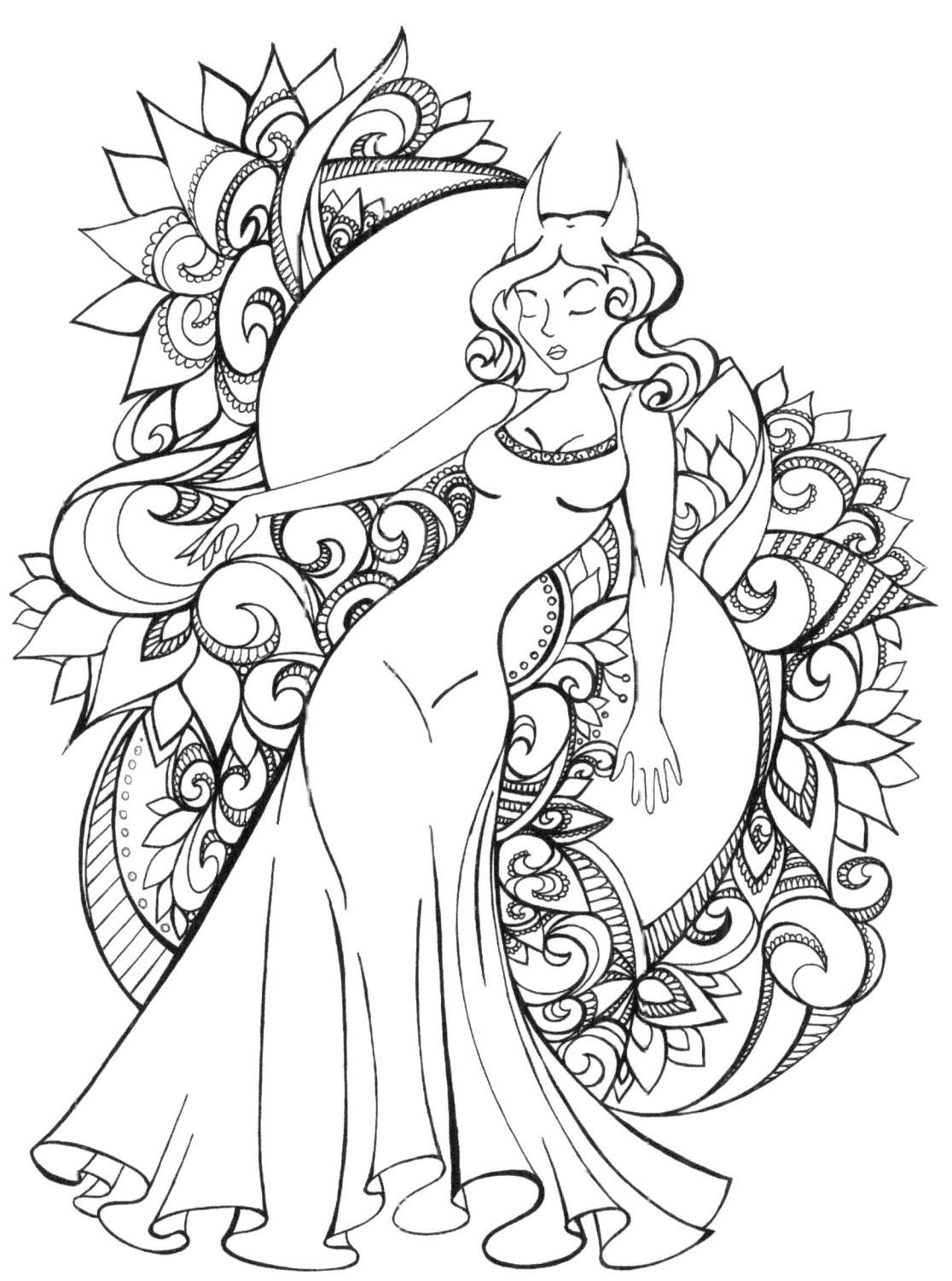

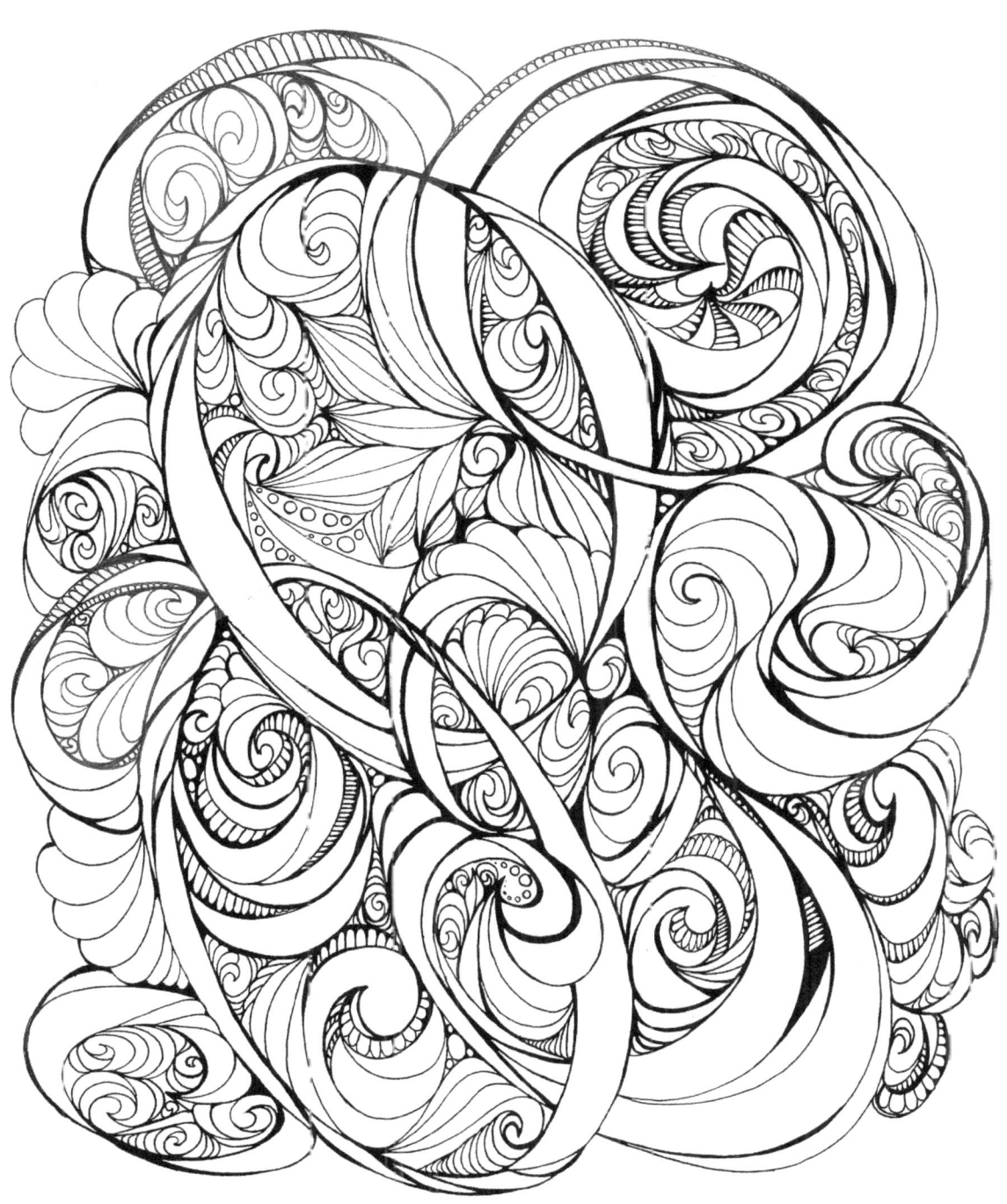

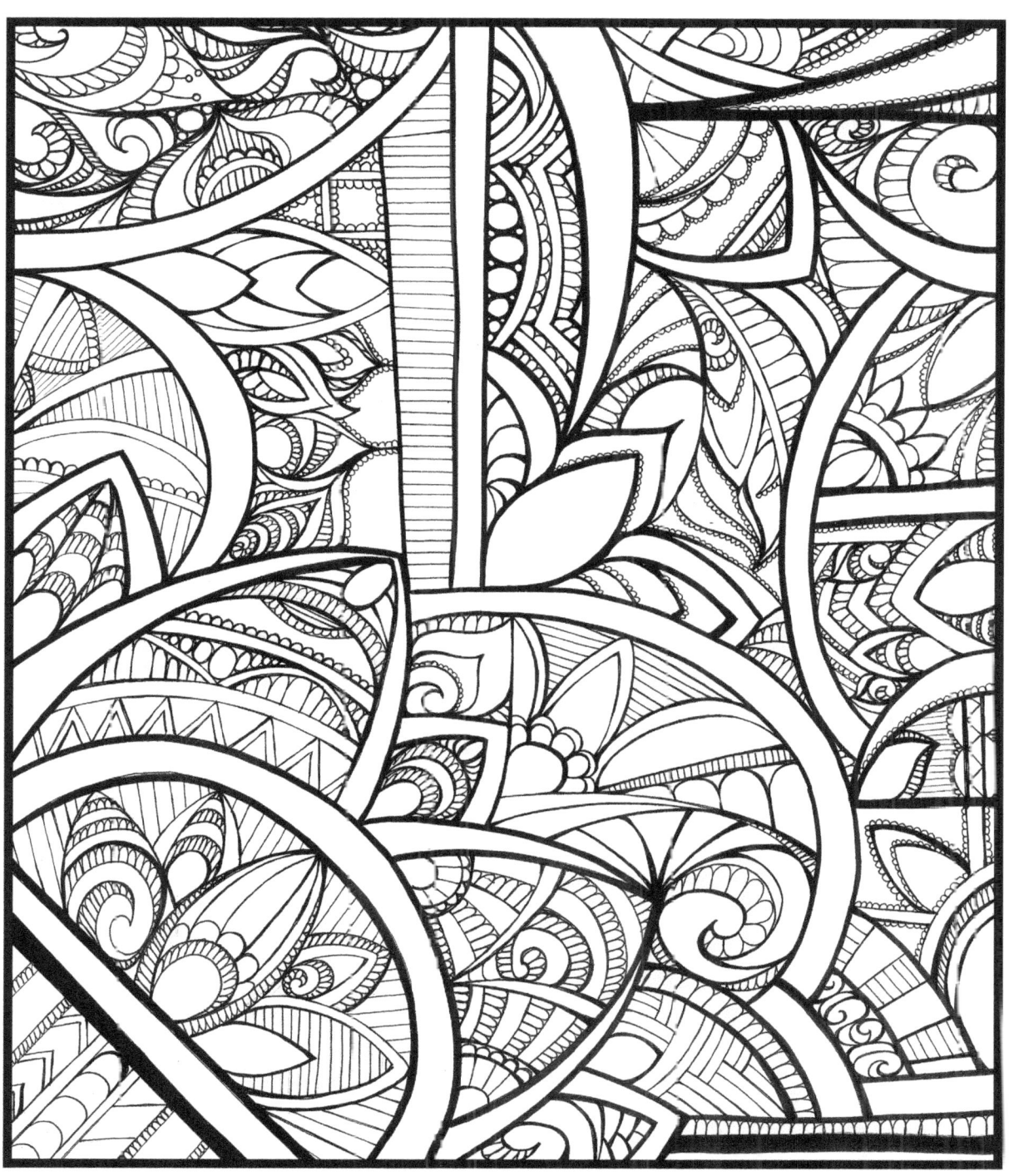

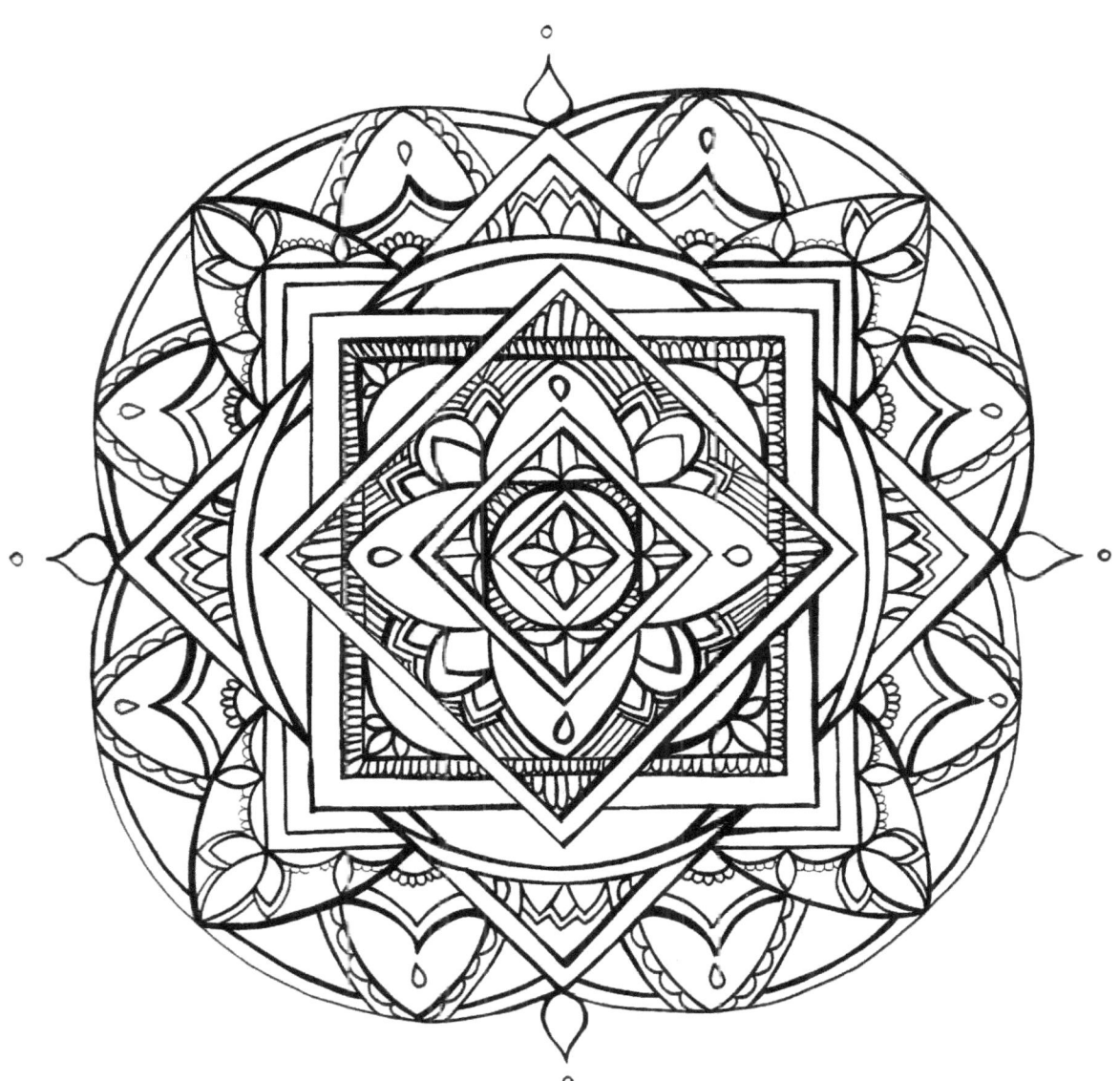

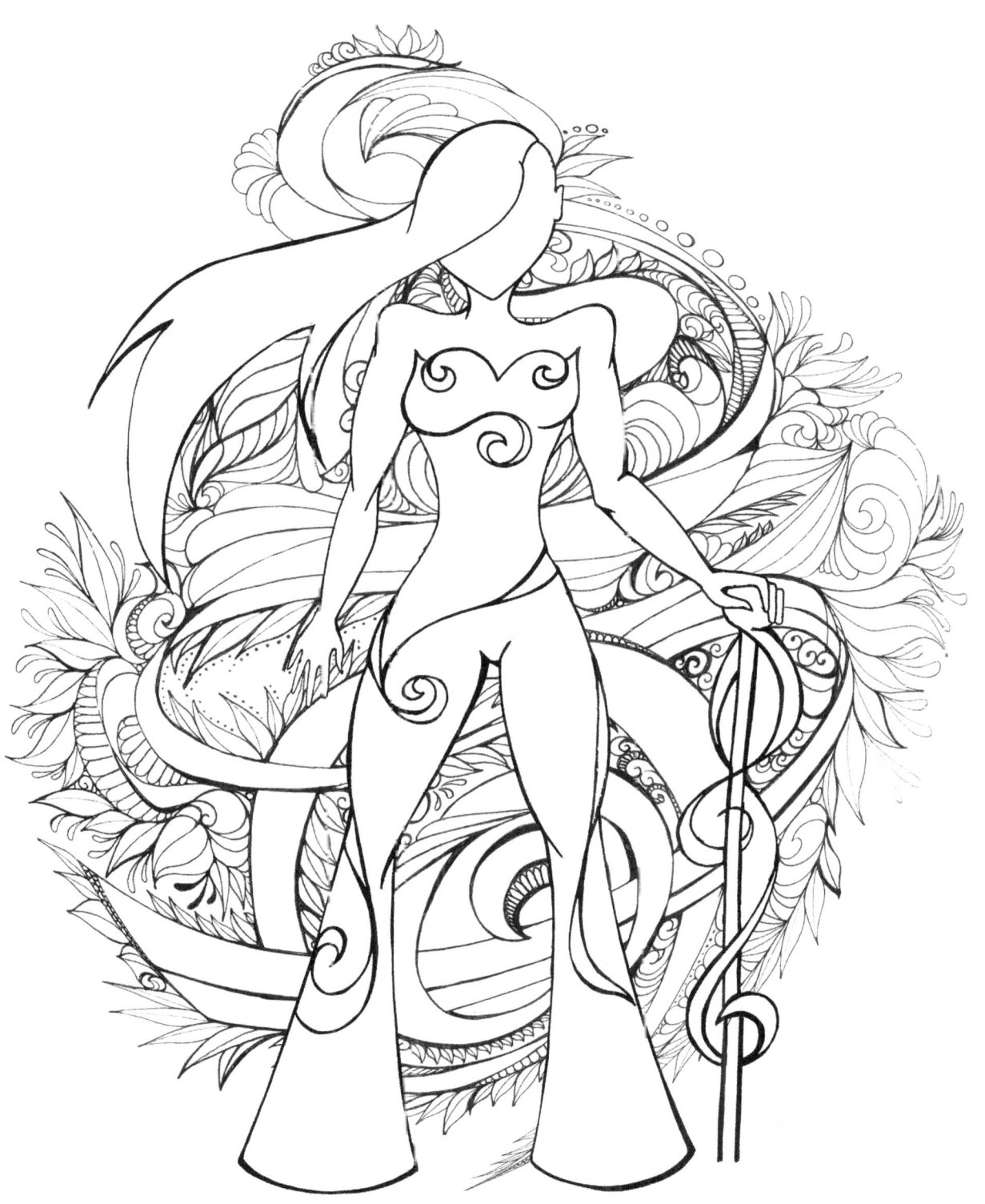

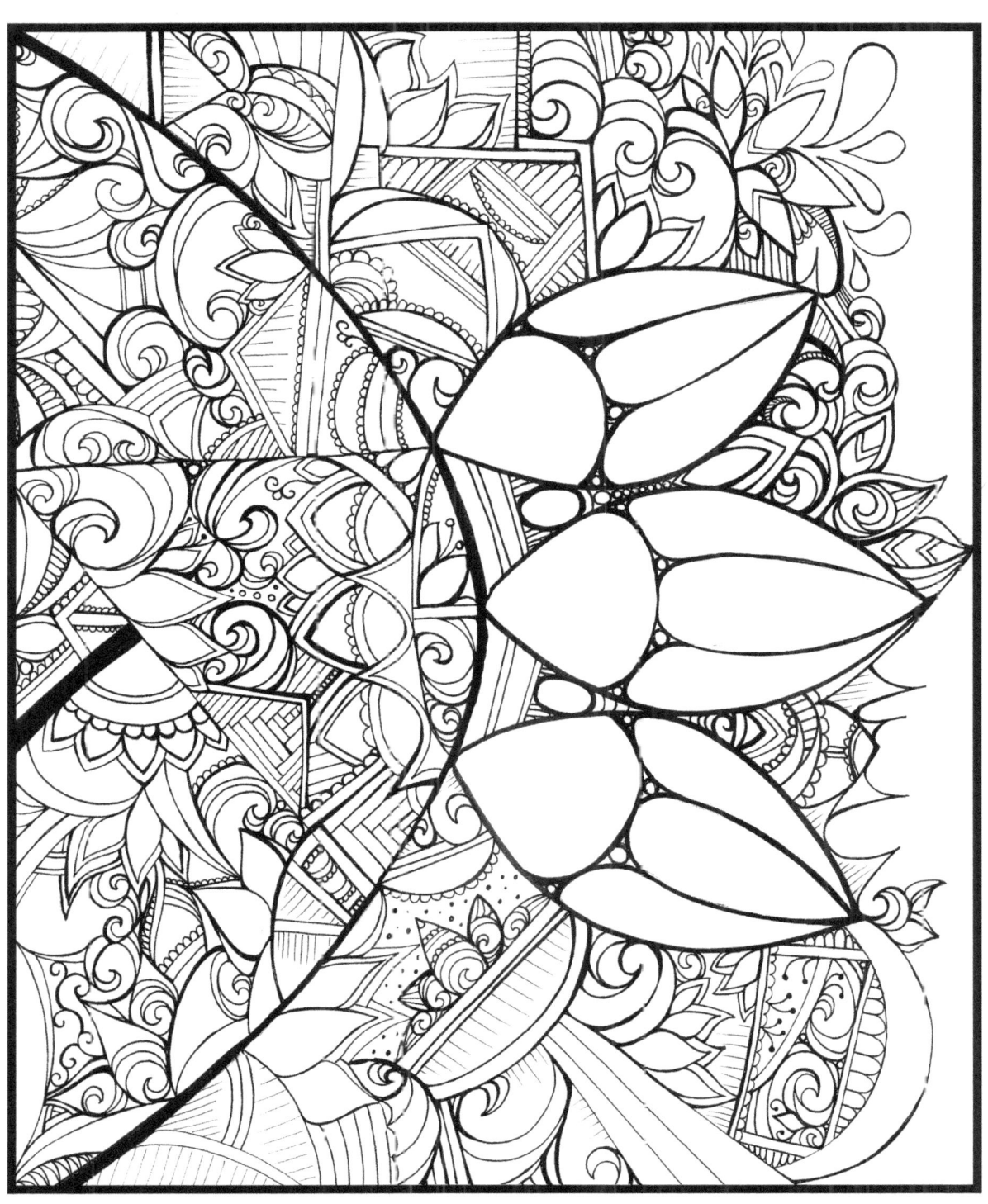

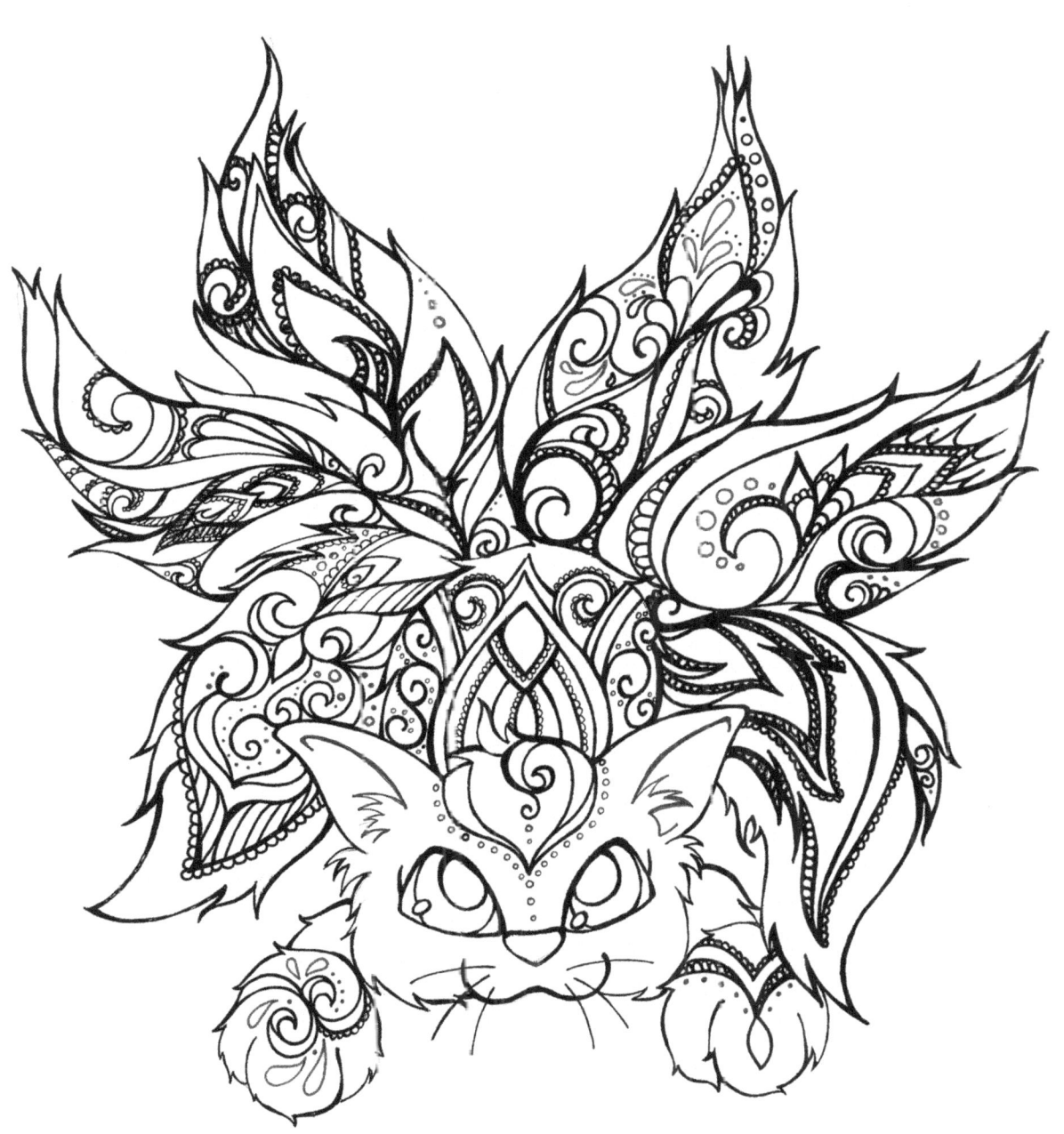

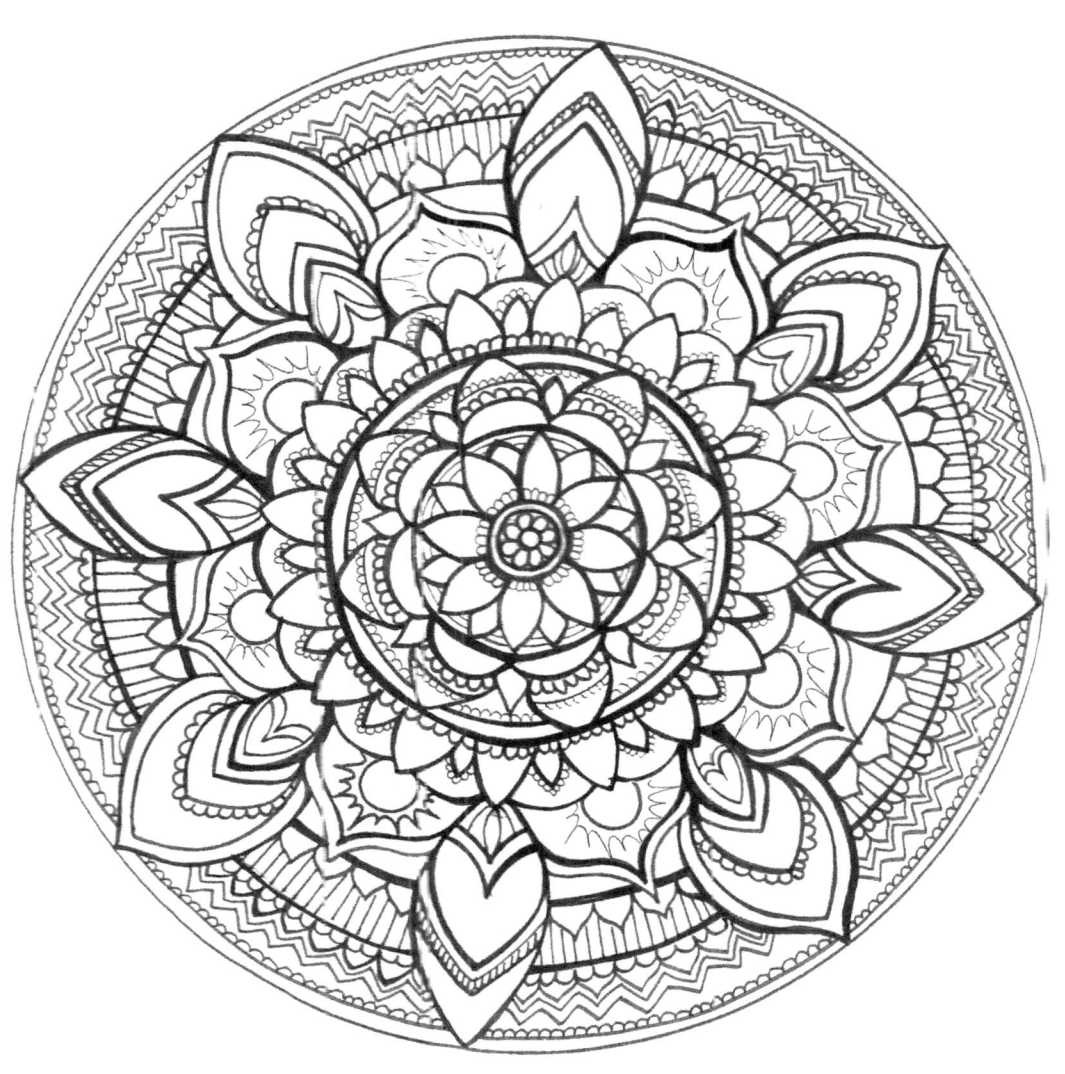

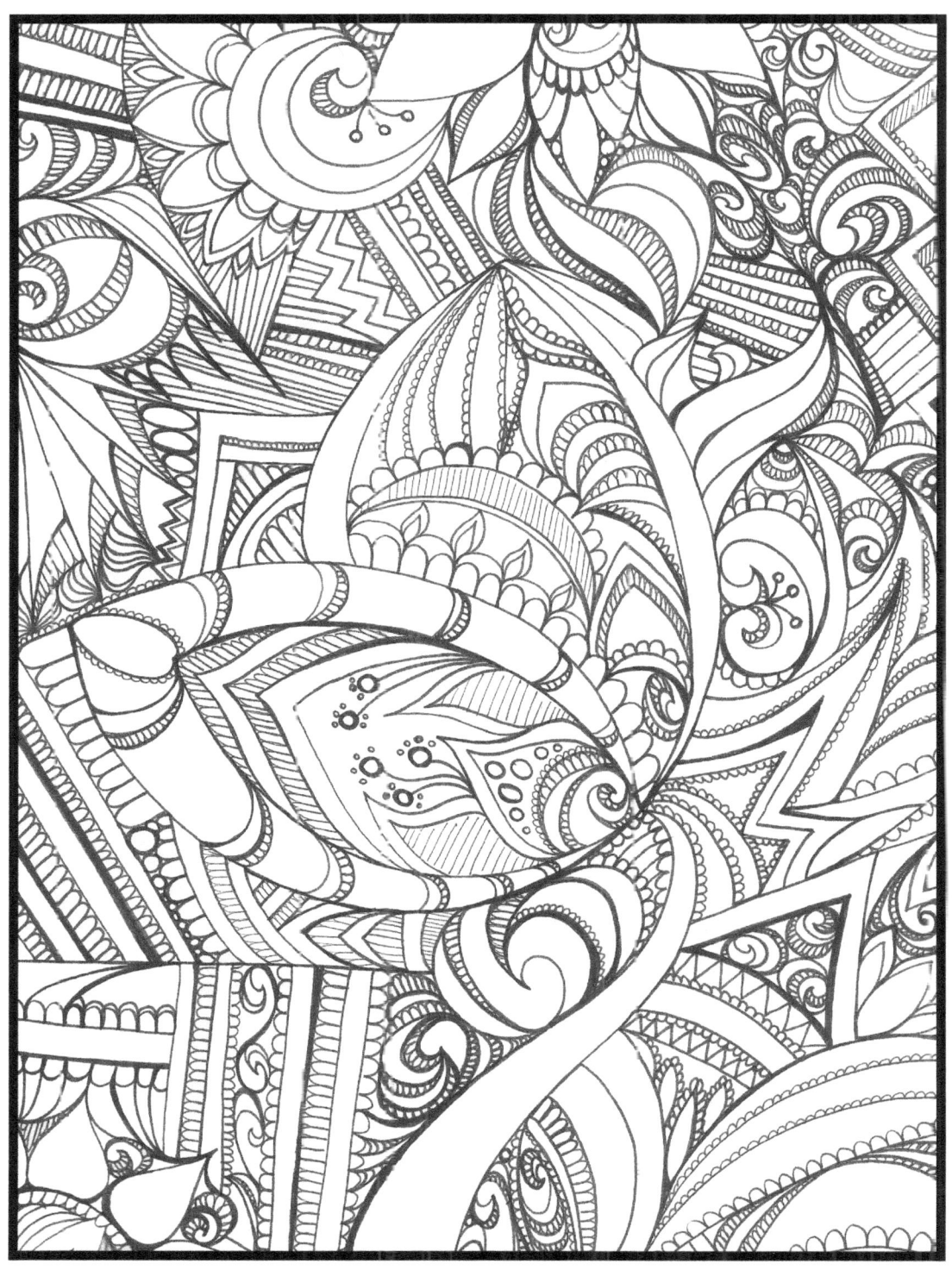

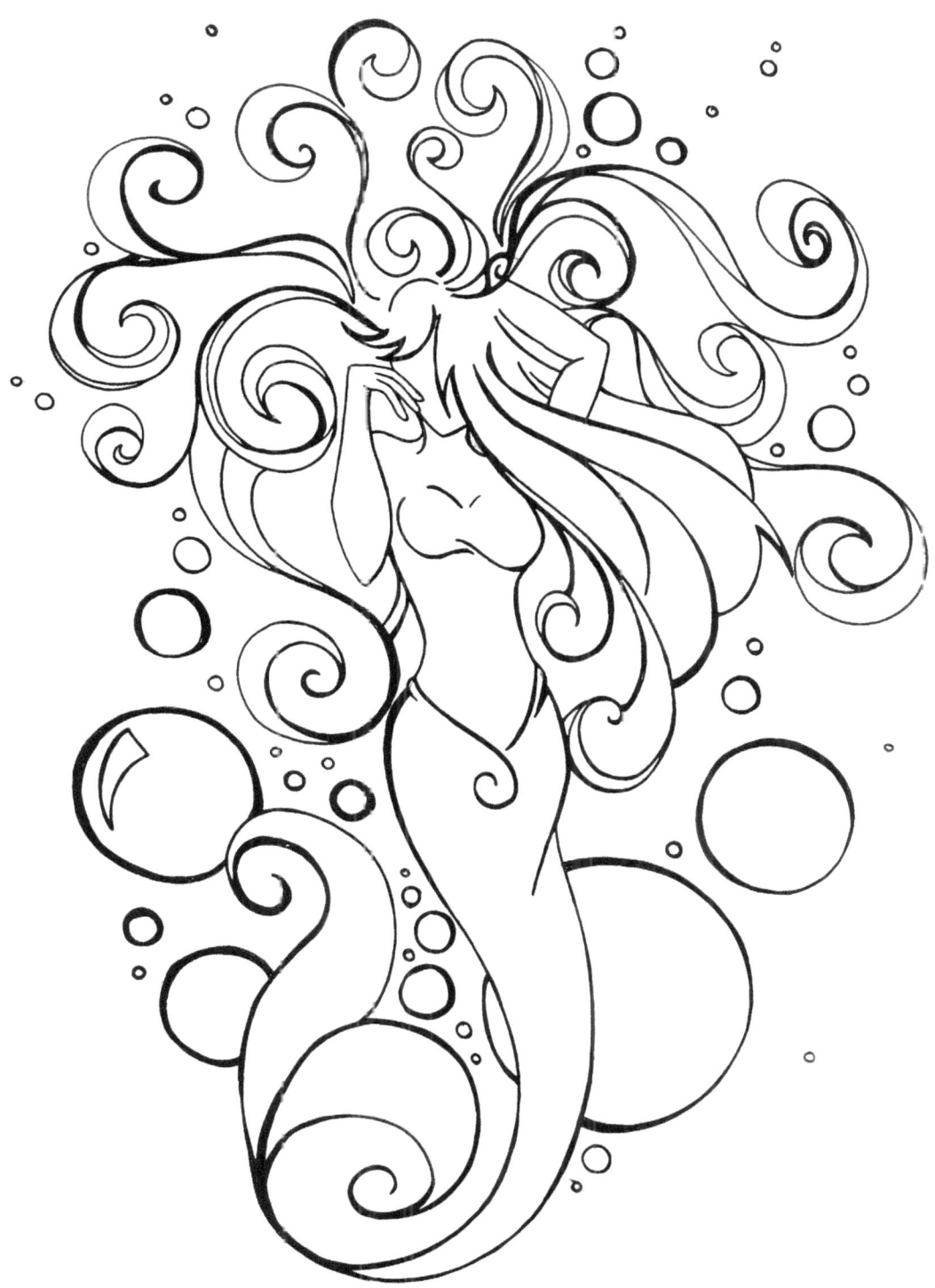

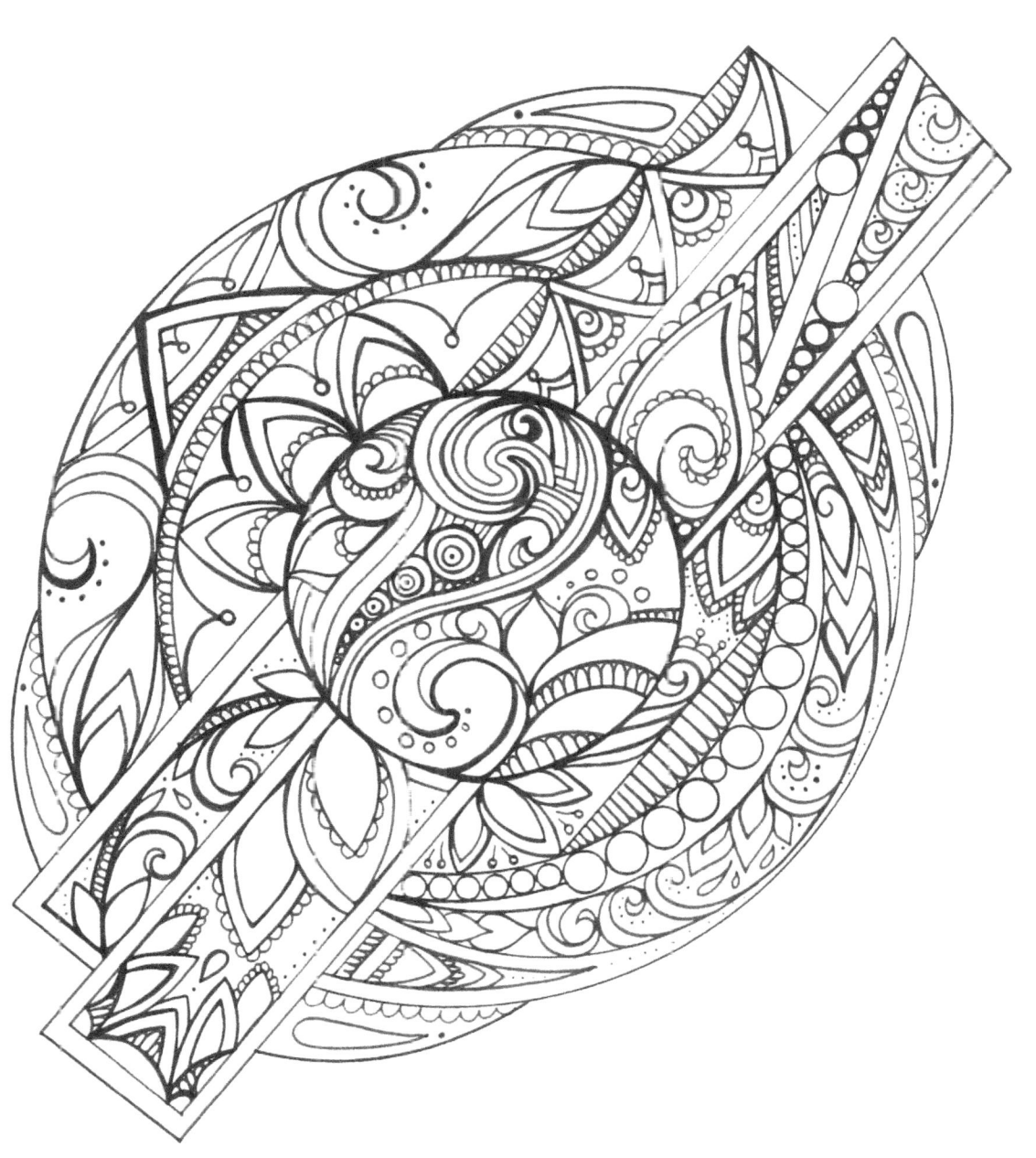

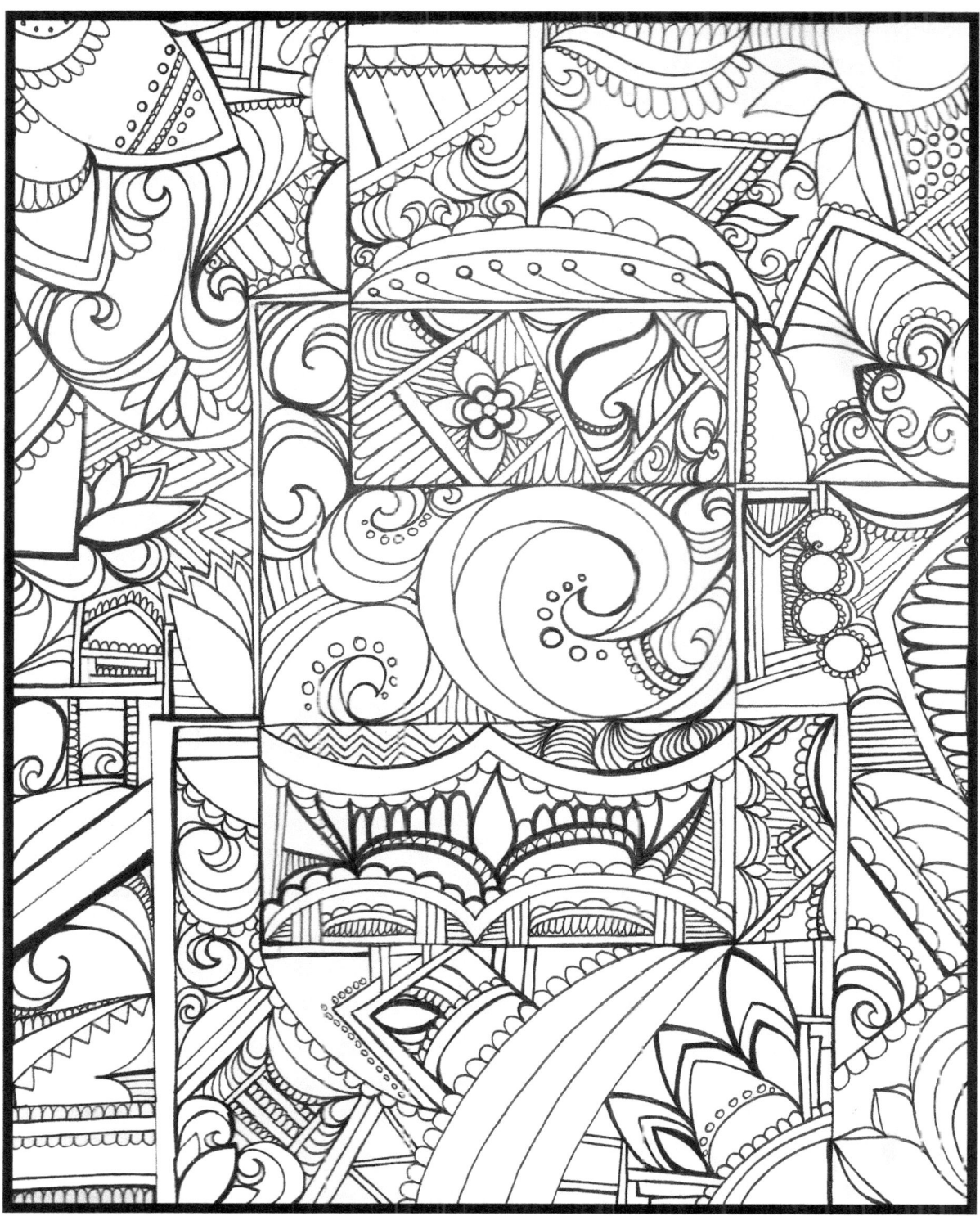

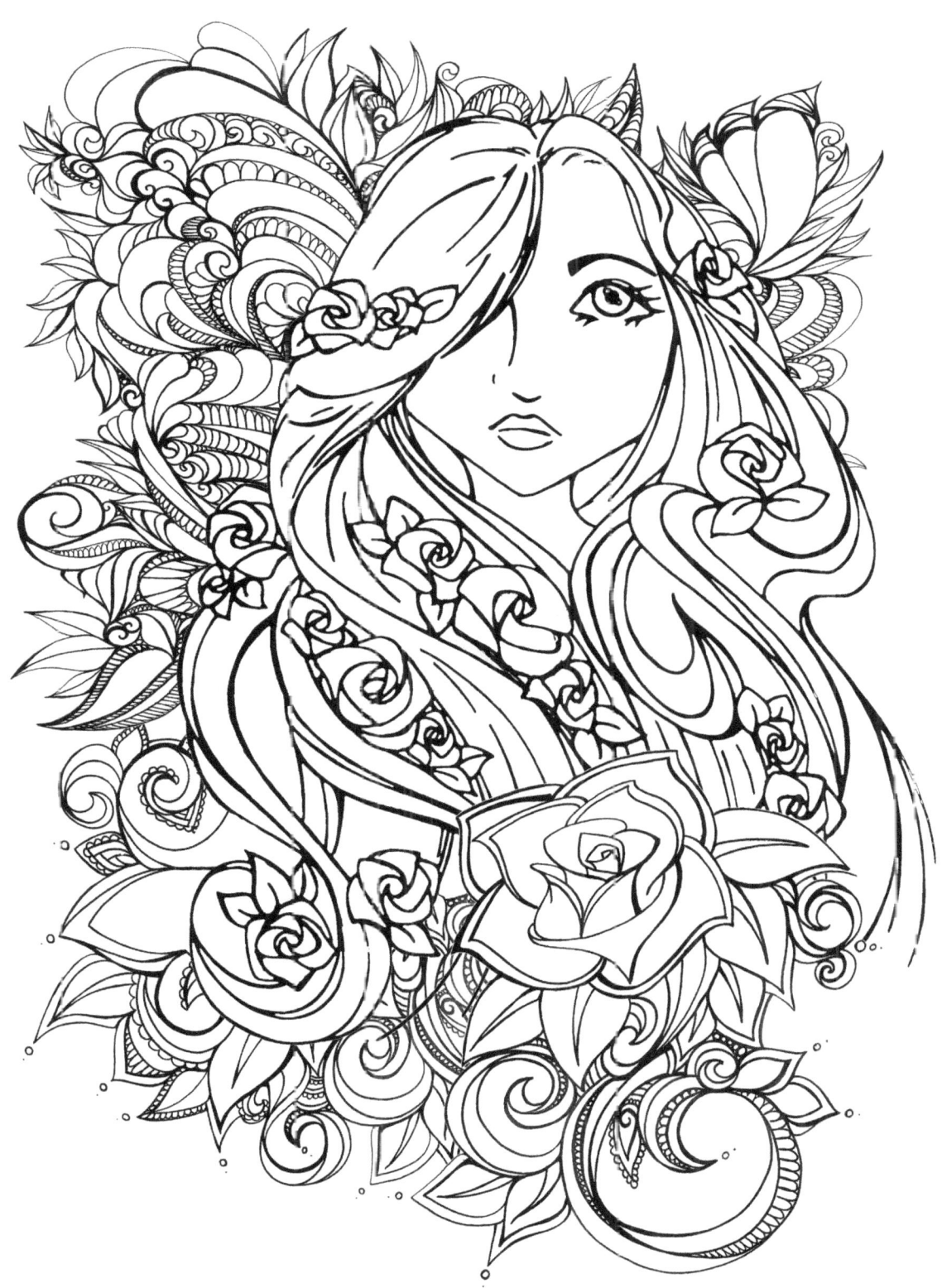

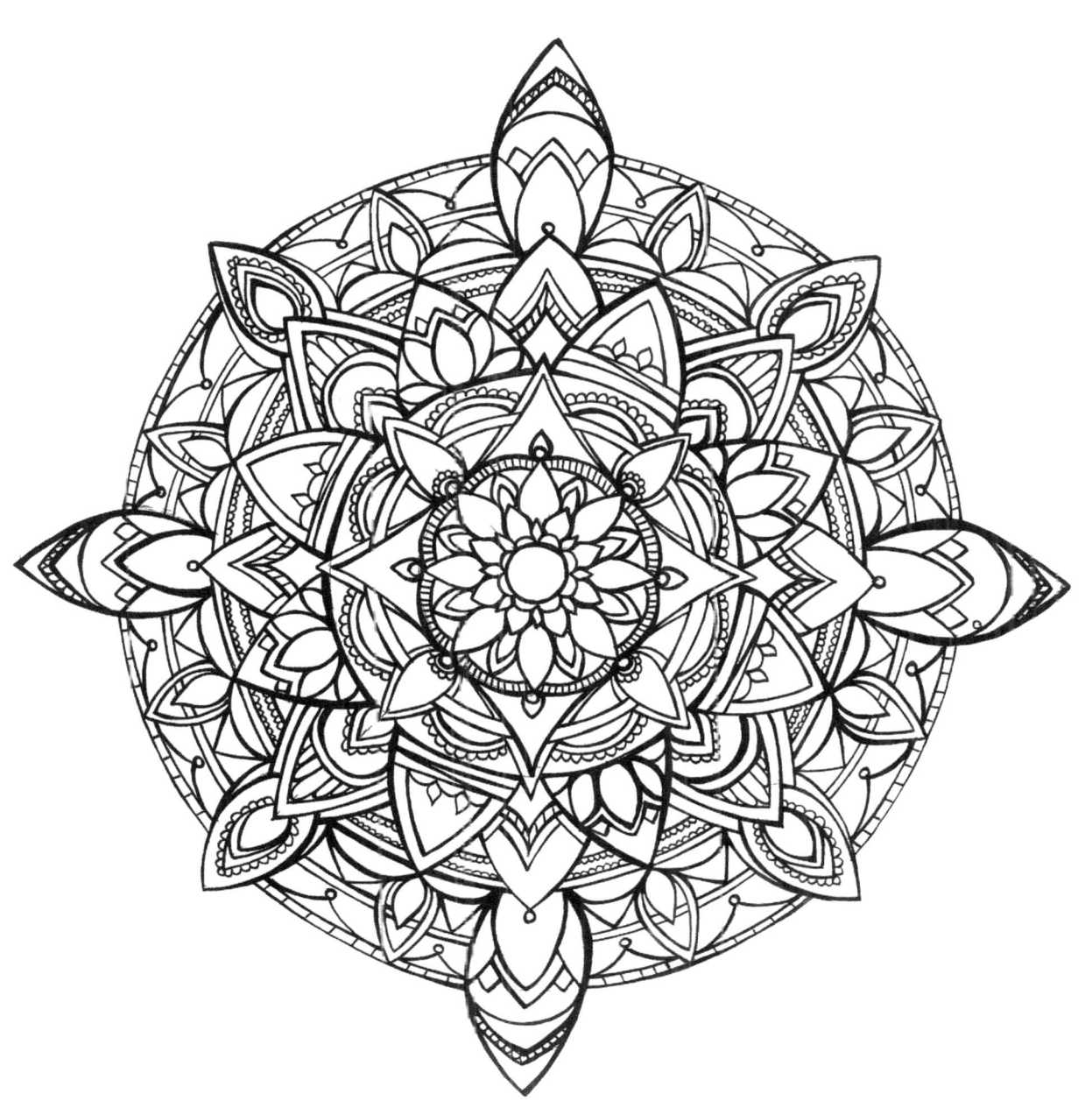

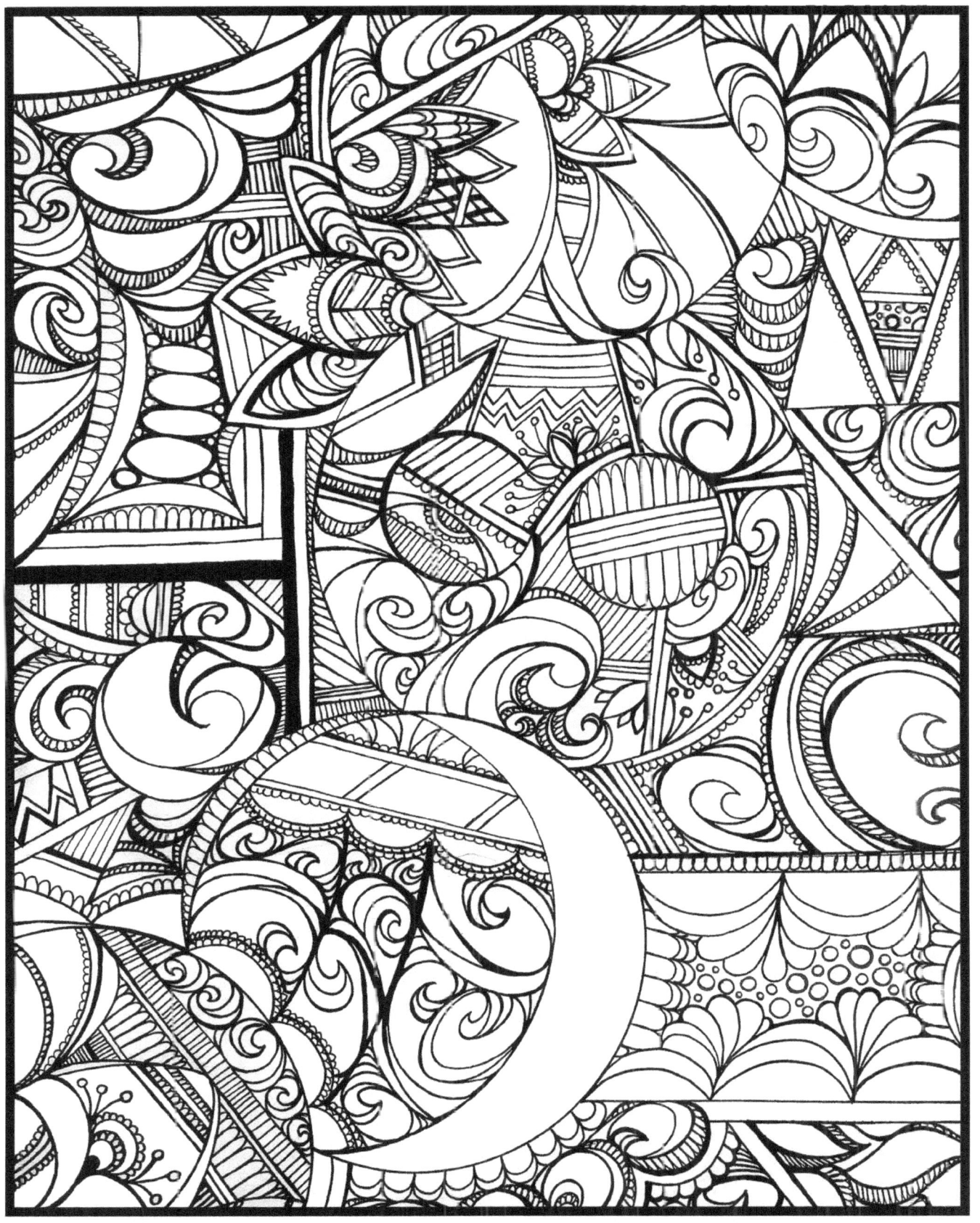

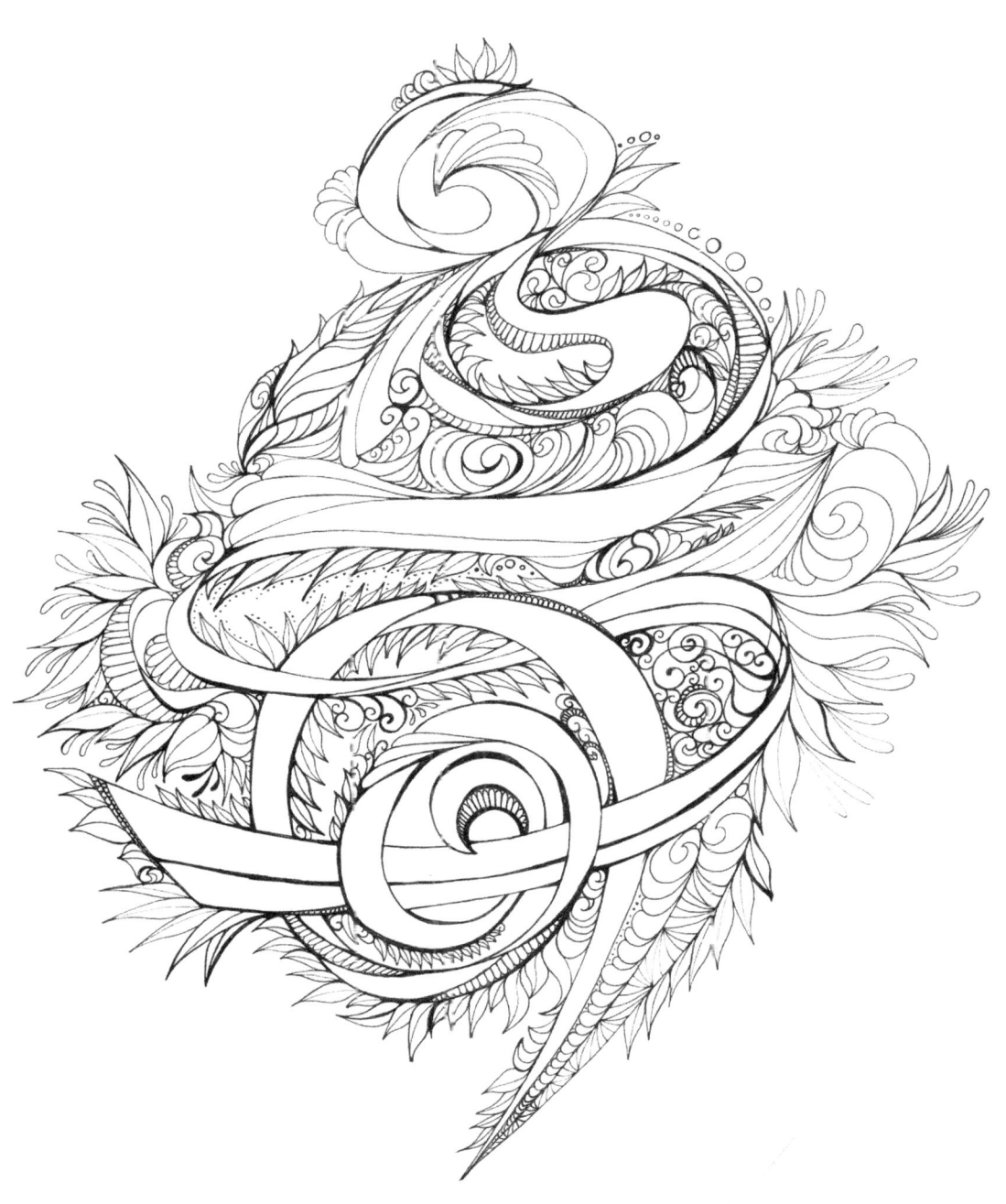

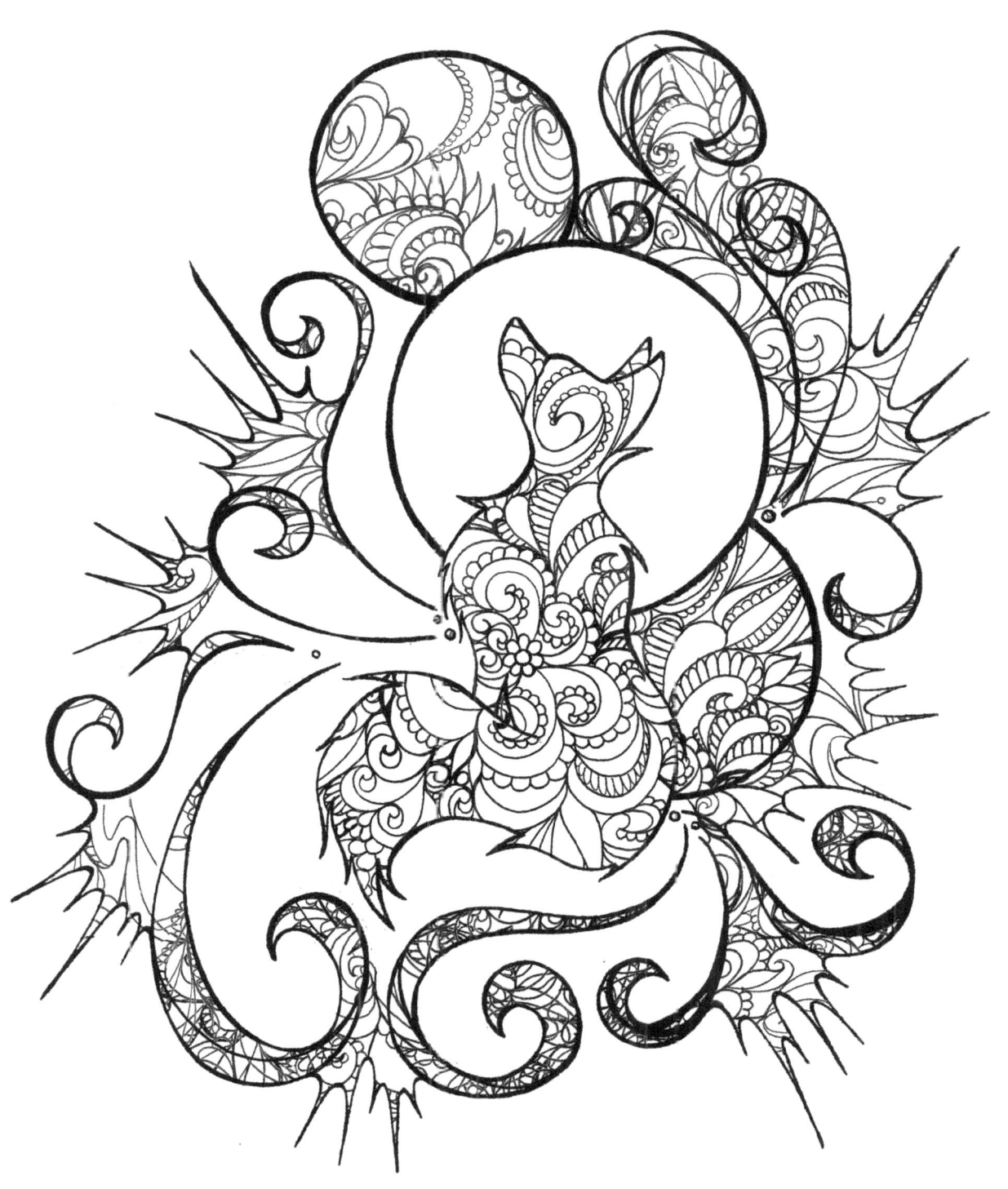

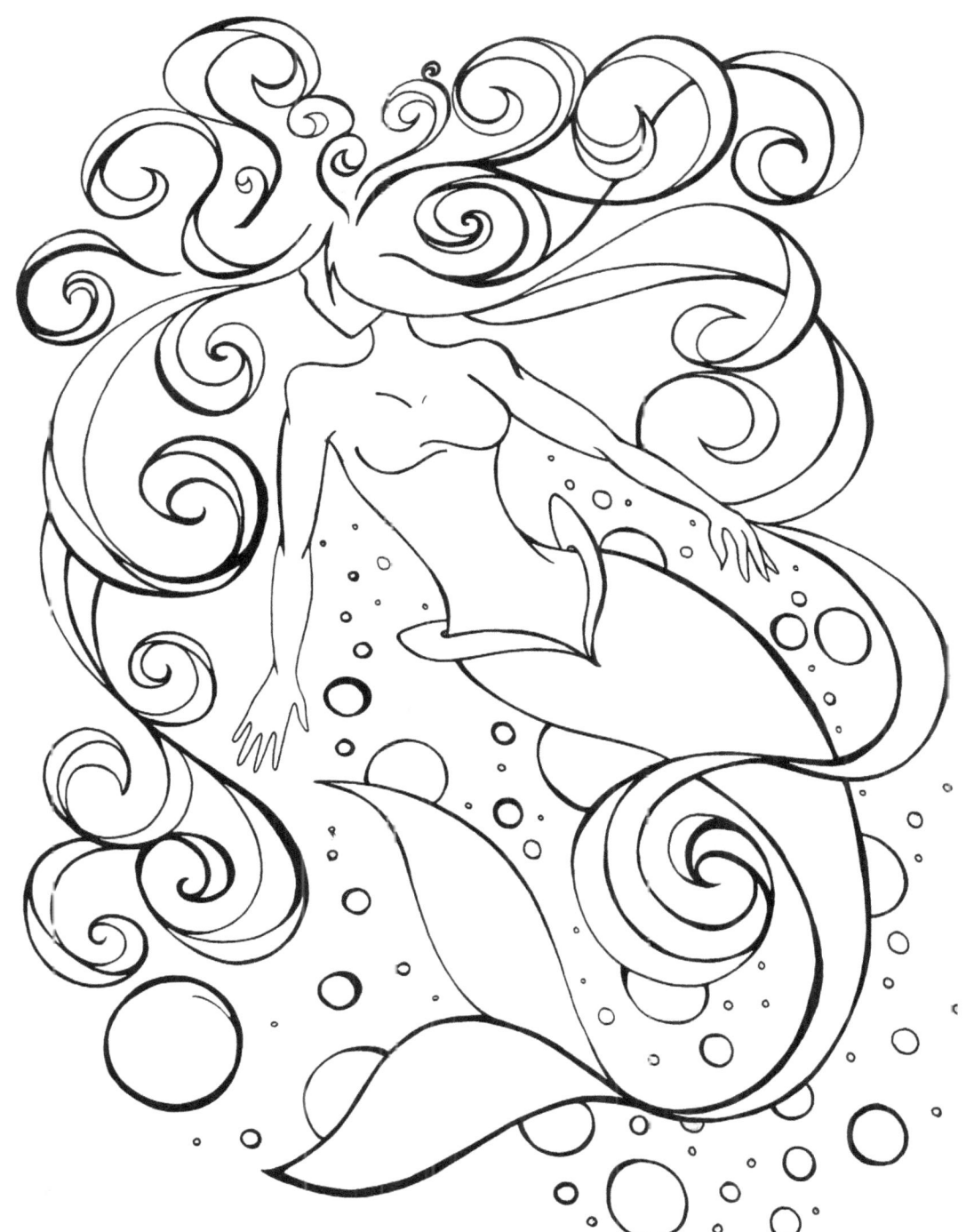

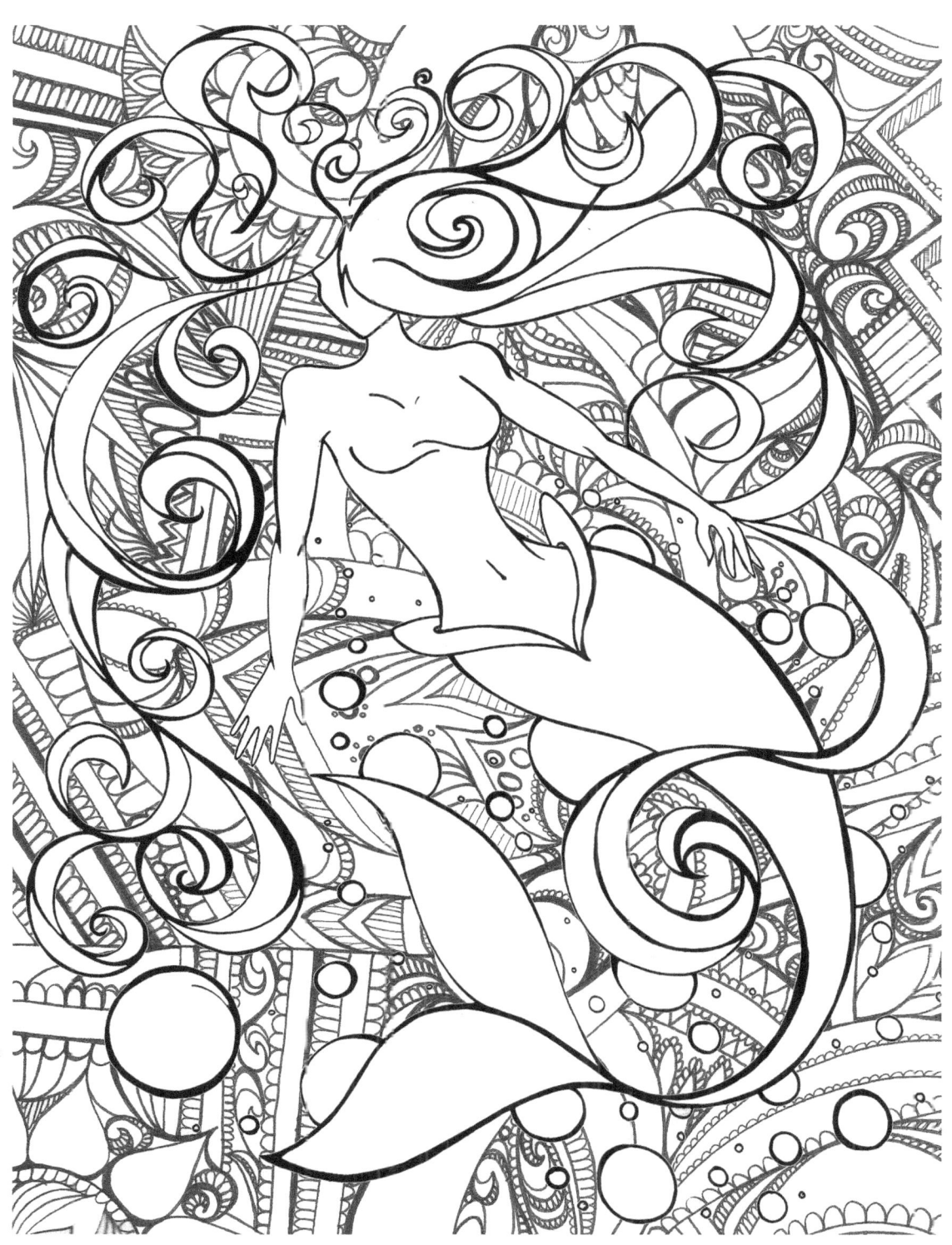

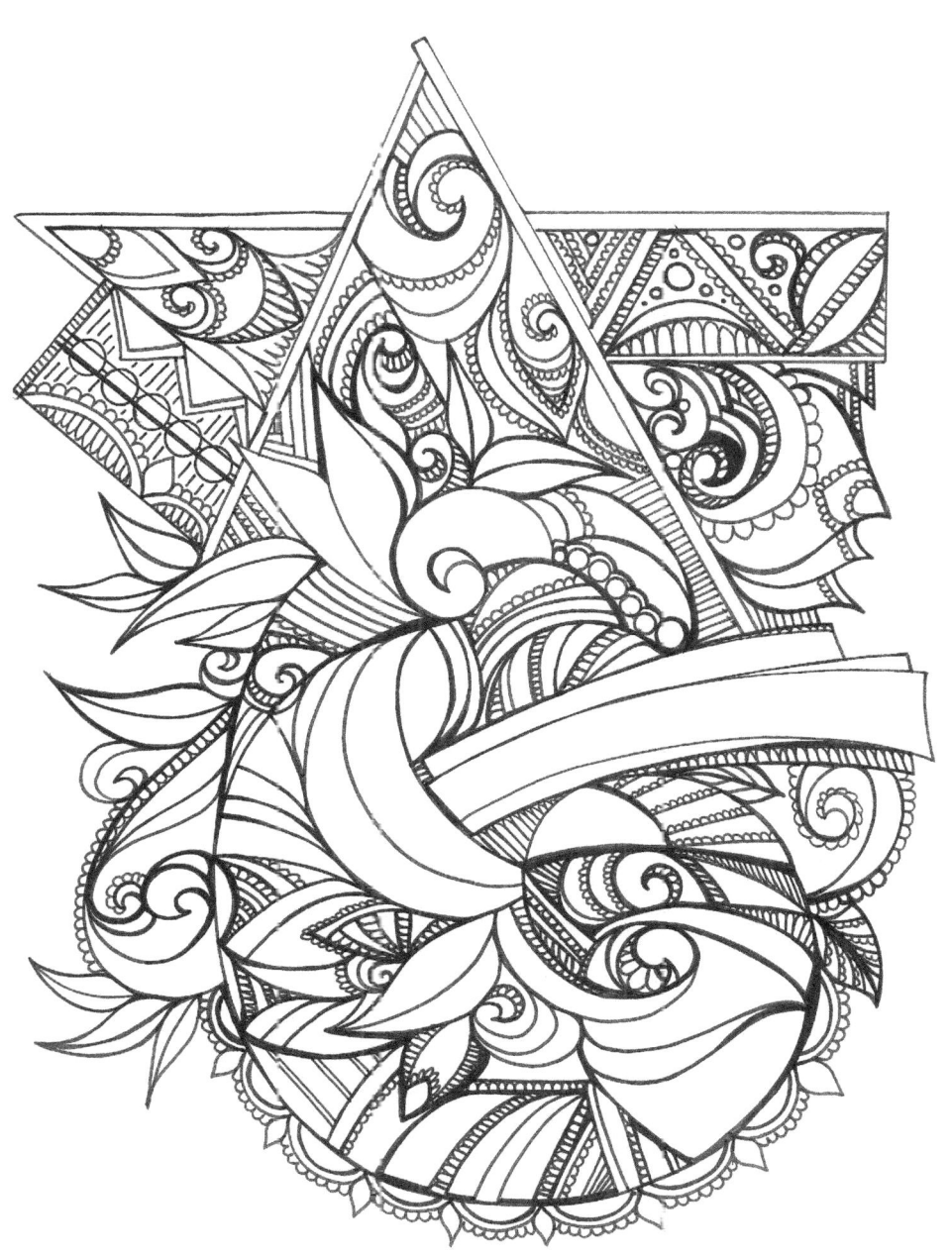

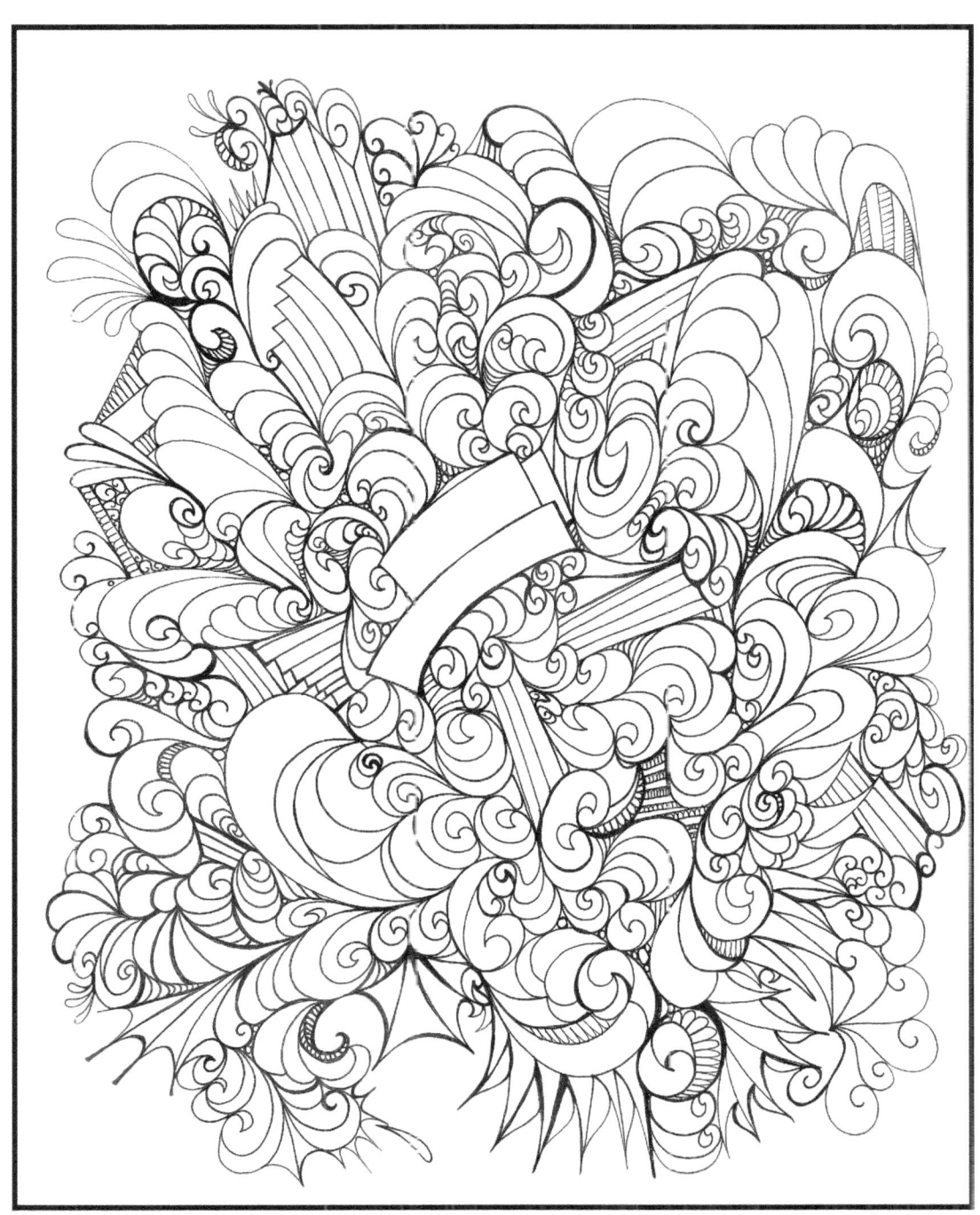

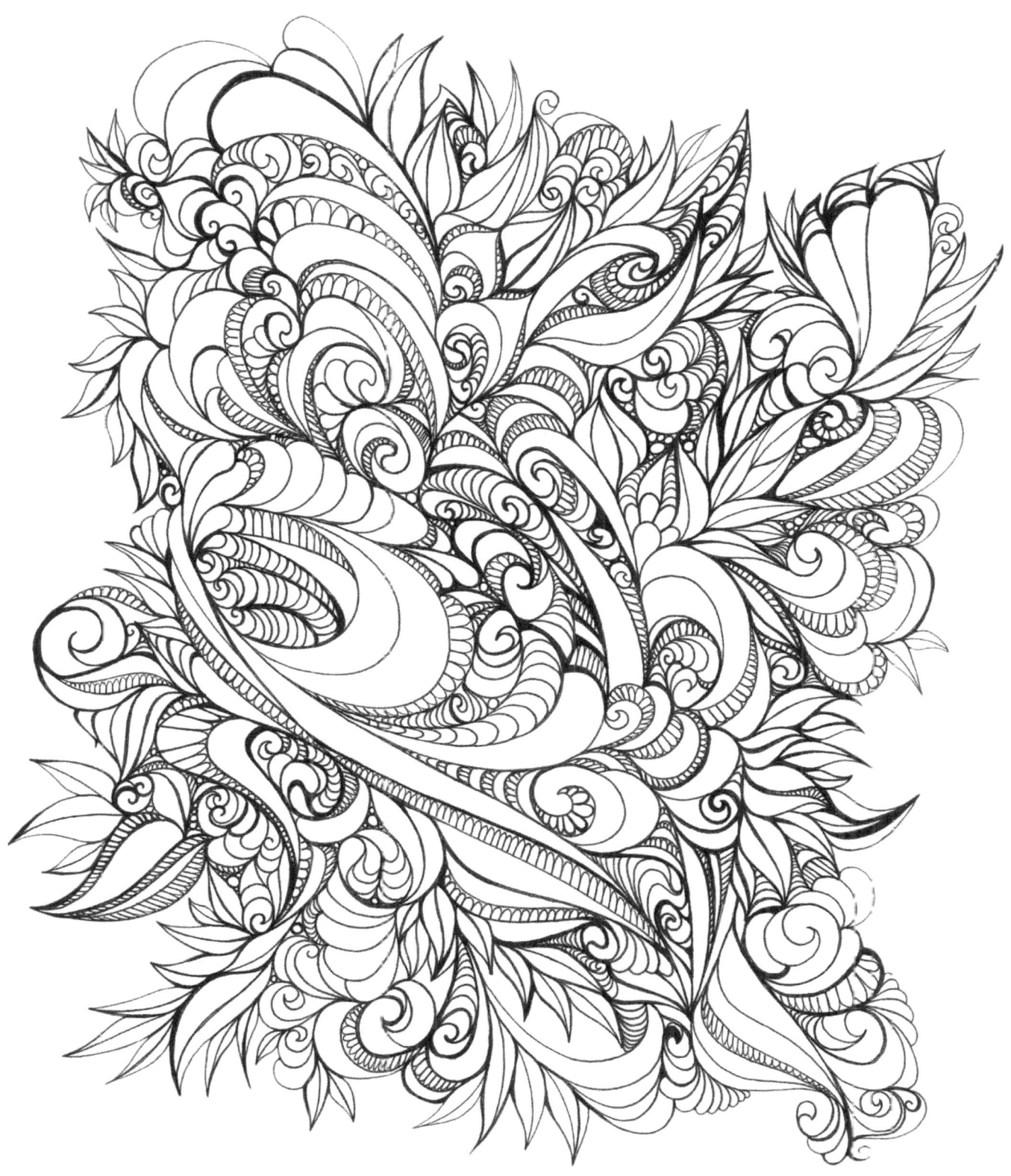

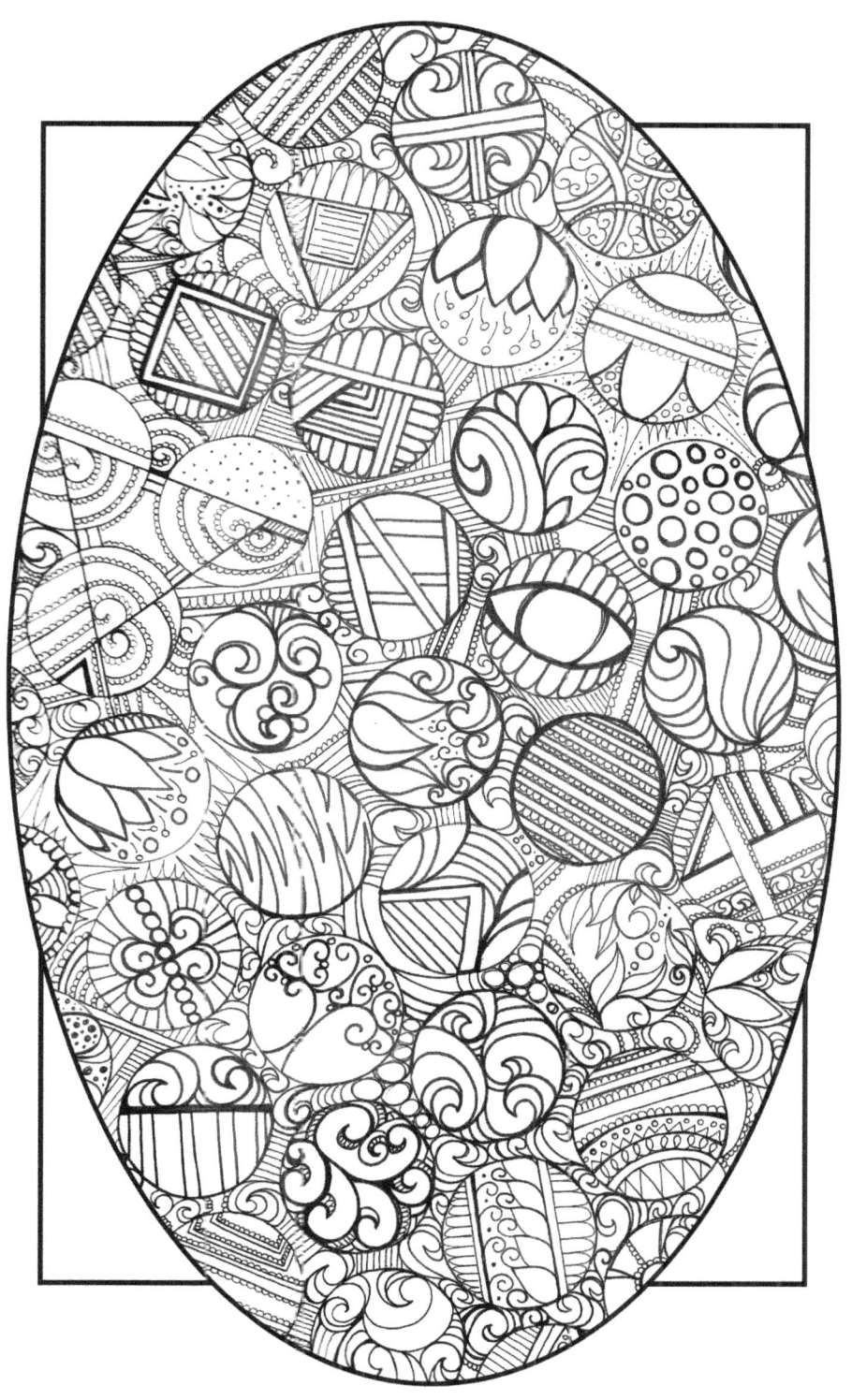

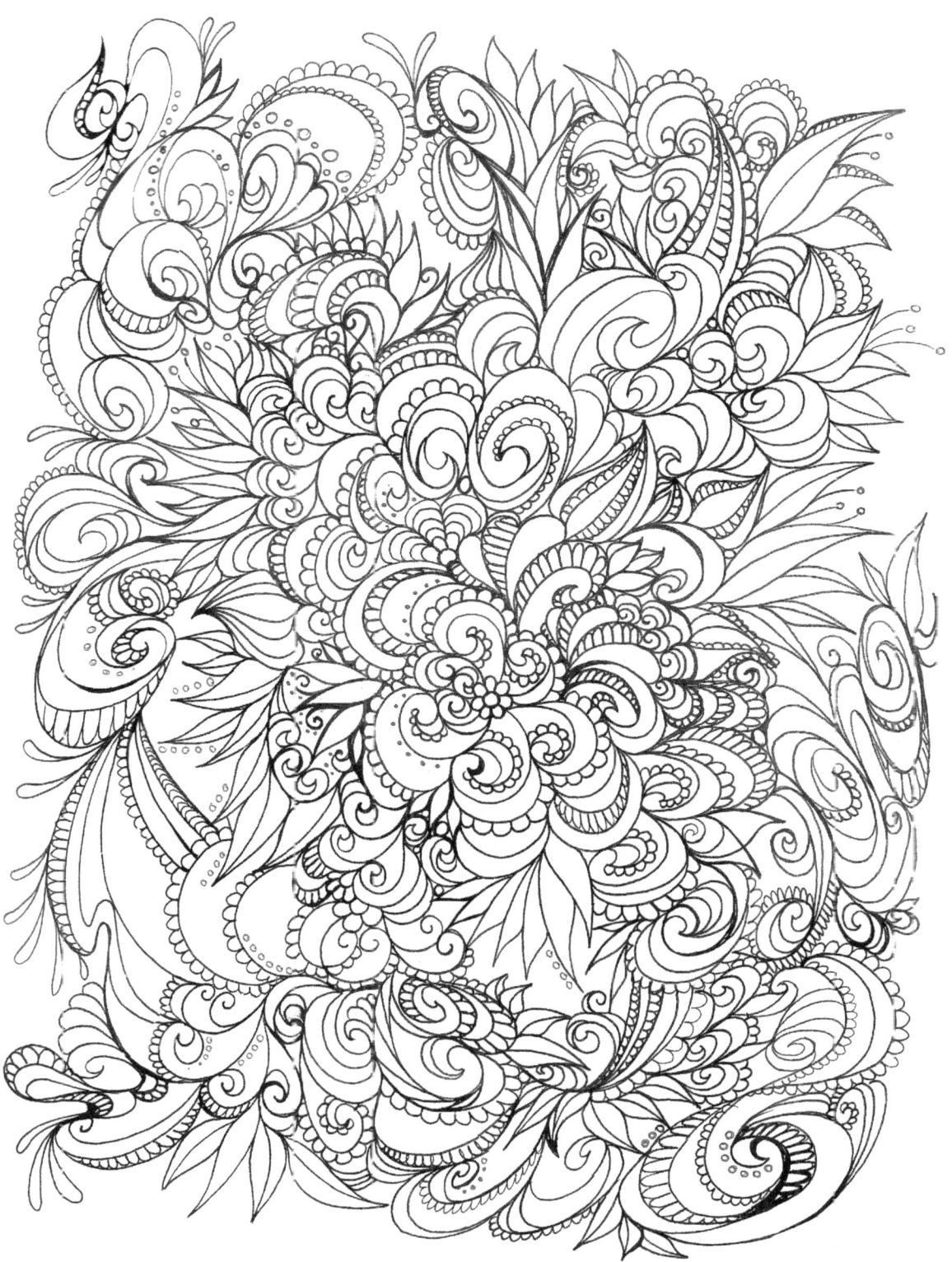

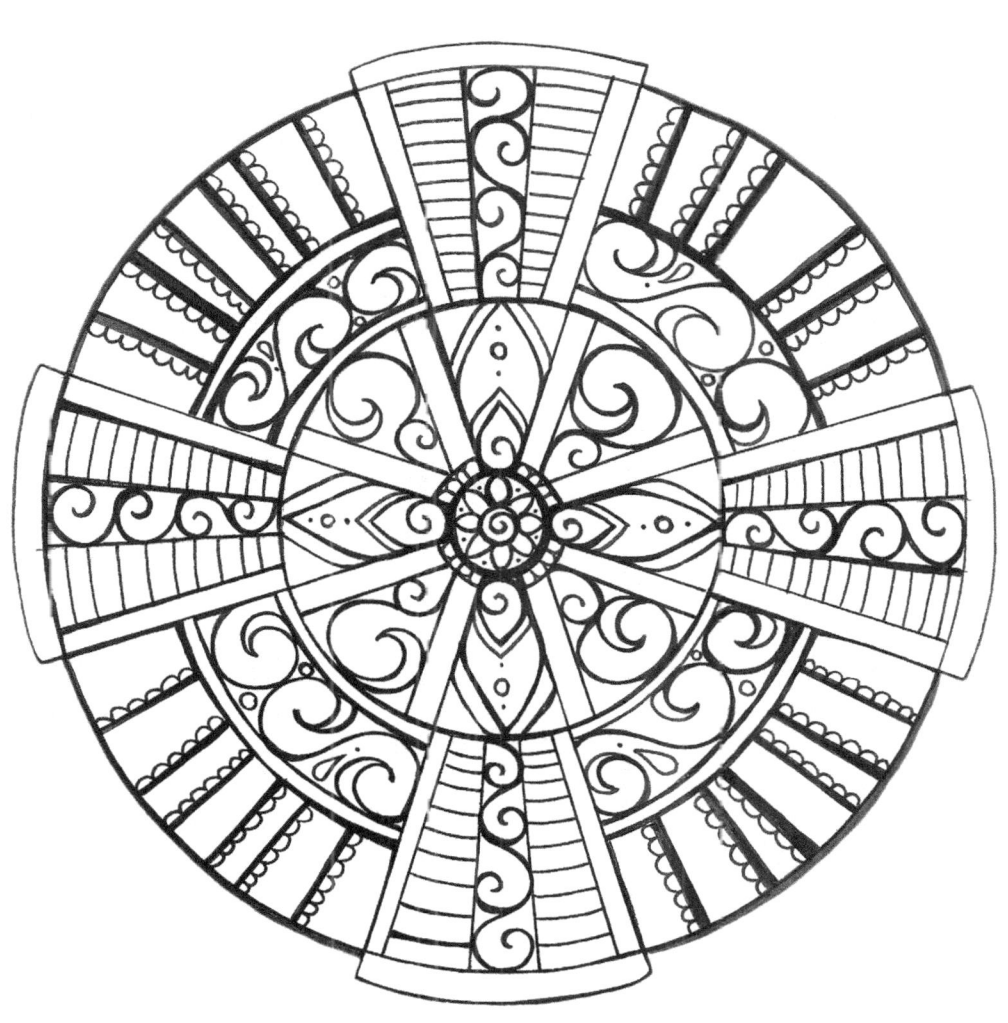

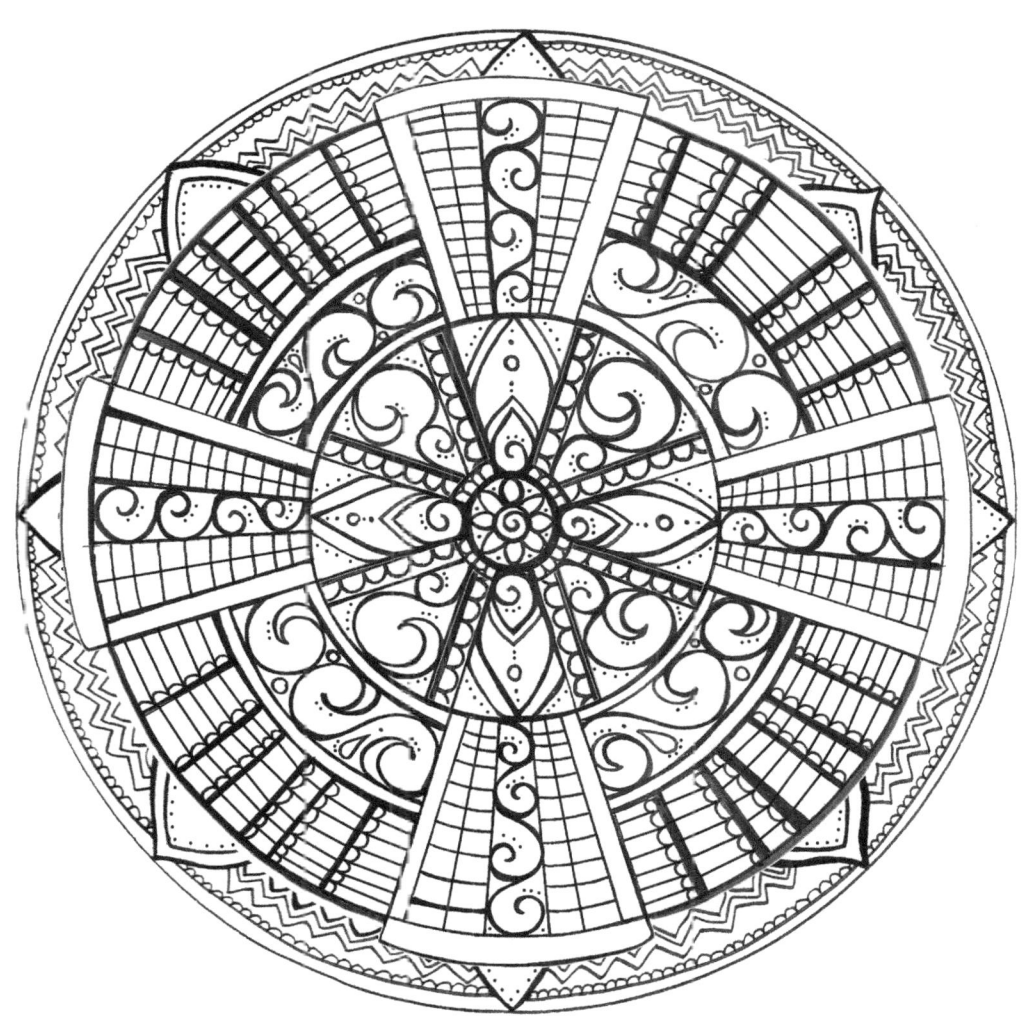

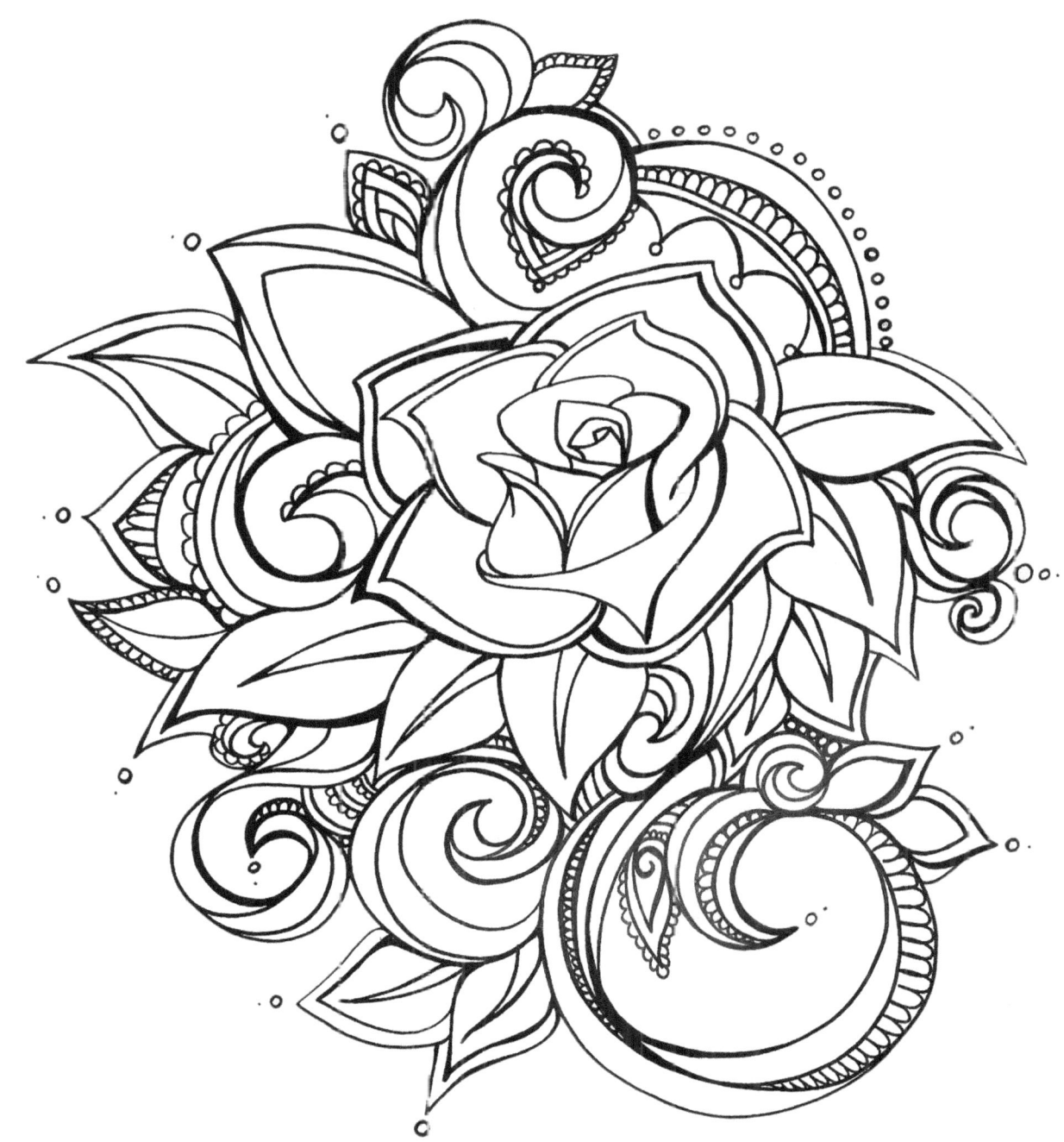

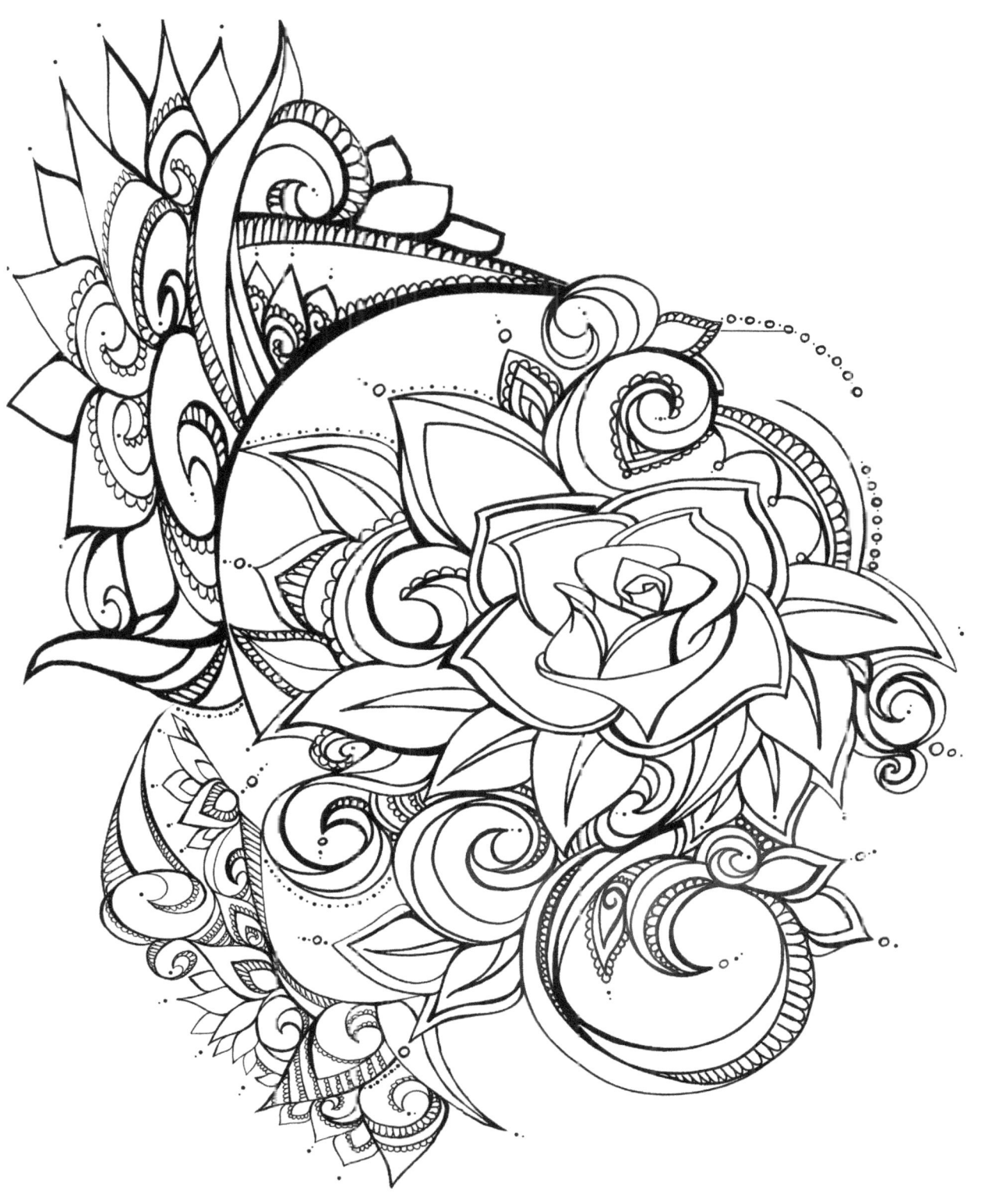

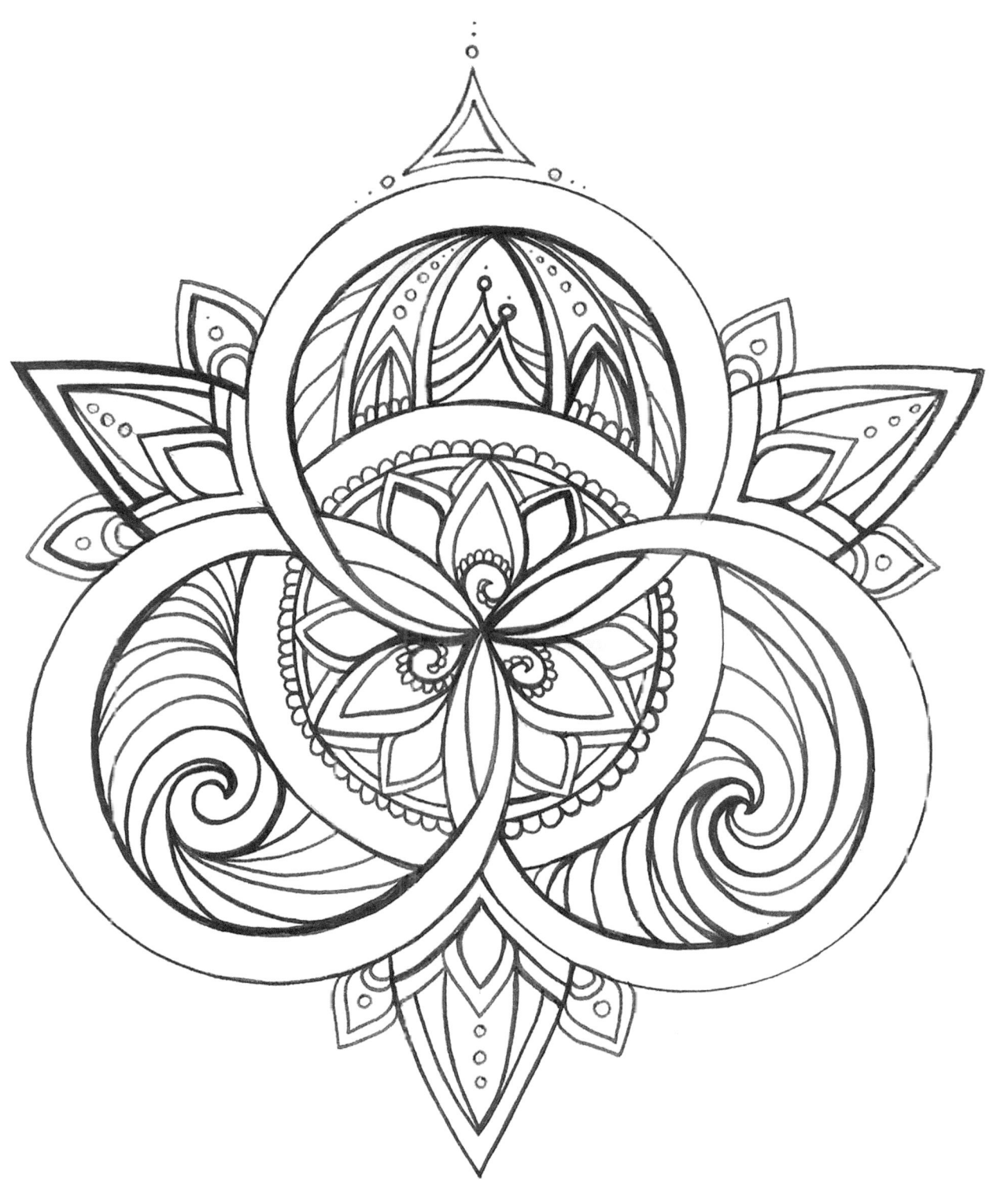

www.ingramcontent.com/pod-product-compliance
Lightning Source LLC
Chambersburg PA
CBHW080543190526
45169CB00007B/2614

* 9 7 8 1 5 3 0 6 6 2 1 4 2 *